For Deanna, Marissa and Gary, in appreciation of their love and support.

And for Linda, who shared the journey.

MY STORY

"The journey of a thousand miles begins with the first step." –Lao Tzu

The Power of Food

I have always been fascinated by the power of food to both heal and harm the human body. I grew up consuming a lot of sugar and very few vegetables. As a young adult, I sensed that my food was making me sick, so I experimented with different kinds of diets. I tried to make better choices to alleviate my chronic eczema and fatigue, improve the quality of my sleep and lose weight. Later on, I became dependent on caffeine to lift my mood and boost my energy throughout the day. I thought I was eating well and exercising sufficiently, but I did not look or feel healthy.

After my daughters were born, my hair started to fall out and I was always tired. They both had immediate symptoms of food allergies and weak immune systems. None of us were seriously ill, but we were not normal in my opinion. This went on for twenty years!

I needed to find a new way to improve my diet and health. In 1999, I enrolled in a vegetarian culinary school, partly because I wanted more knowledge about expanding my food choices, but also to learn how to replace meat, dairy, wheat, eggs and other foods with alternatives that were just as healthy—or maybe even more so. This gave me a new way of thinking and eating that had the potential to dramatically change my health. I also learned from my education, and later from my coaching experience, that what is healthy for one person may not be for another—and that our bodies often give us feedback about what's good or bad for us.

In 2010, my family members and I finally attained state-of-the-art testing for gluten intolerance and food allergies. Being diagnosed with gluten and dairy sensitivities was the best bad news we have ever received. It solved the mystery of which foods were the source of our problems. It set us on a path of healing and self-awareness. During the transition process, I didn't just give up the old foods all at once; instead, I slowly replaced them with healthier versions of foods that satisfied the same needs and desires. My diet makeover, which evolved over several years, also required a greater proportion of vegetables, whole grains and protein, and a lesser amount of sugar and processed food. This multi-step experience has informed my current work as a health coach, allowing me to support my clients as they change their habits and their lives.

As time goes on, I know that if I eat well, get enough exercise and participate in activities that I enjoy, *I am less attracted to unhealthy food and can stay in control of my health.* The journey is never completely over for any of us, but if you figure out your *recipe for a healthy life,* it is the best way to ensure that you will continue to be happy and healthy.

THE RECIPE FOR A
HEALTHY LIFE COOKBOOK

Is this your story?

- You are stuck eating the same foods and want a simple approach to lose weight or improve your health.

- You are often tired and depend on sugar and caffeine to boost your energy and your mood.

- You have a gluten intolerance, food allergy or medical condition that requires a special diet, but you struggle to maintain it.

- You don't always eat well because of stress or a busy schedule.

- You lack the knowledge or confidence to cook a variety of vegetables, whole grains and nutritious snacks that the whole family can enjoy.

Are you open to change?

It doesn't have to be complicated or difficult to eat and live well. If you are open to slowly incorporating new wholesome foods into your routine, and willing to expand your diet with a variety of flavors and combinations, you will be able to get yourself on a healthy path. It can be that simple and can be achieved on your own timetable. If you are patient and trust that your body will respond to nourishing fuel, you will gradually see results in your health and wellbeing. It can be a subtle, yet powerful transformation.

This book is intended to give you the guidance to improve your diet and your lifestyle. When you do more of your own cooking, eat less processed food and depend less on restaurants, you reclaim a measure of control over your health each day and for the future. This book will help you to cultivate a mindset to try new foods, learn new skills in the kitchen, and apply time-management tools to support your dietary goals that will survive the test of time.

Changing your habits could change your life.

As a certified health coach and professionally trained chef, I enjoy the challenge of helping people to discover which foods improve their health, are easy to prepare, and taste good. In my experience, most people are doing the best they can to eat and live well, given their busy lifestyles and lack of familiarity with other food options. However, they struggle with their weight, fatigue, sleep, digestion, sugar cravings, food allergies and much more. We live in a world that's overloaded with information on food and health topics, making it difficult for individuals to sort out what kind of diet would help them reach their goals, and how to implement it. Where should people begin?

This book provides a practical and easy way to start learning about the benefits of whole foods and what particular diet or combination of foods is right for you. It takes time and experimentation to find the food that you enjoy preparing and eating, and that makes you feel like your best self.

My Views

My views of diet and health are based on personal and professional experience, formal education and my own research. The information and recipes in this book are intended to be a guide and an inspiration. If something resonates with you or raises a concern, I encourage you to do your own research, seek guidance from a trusted health professional, or contact me to discuss it further.

My intention is to expose readers to new ideas, or reframe general knowledge in a way that is memorable and easy to implement. No matter how healthy or adept in the kitchen you consider yourself to be, there is always room to fine-tune or improve a little bit. It's not about being perfect, because you'll never get there. But you can continually try new food and new recipes, and tune in to your own physical needs.

A Healthy Diet:

- Makes you look and feel great, and can slowly lead you toward an optimal weight and increased self-confidence.

- Helps you to wake up every morning feeling rested, with steady energy throughout the day.

- Does not produce the digestive discomfort of acid reflux, gas, bloating, constipation or pain.

- Reduces cravings for sugar or caffeine.

- Does not cause you to eat too little or too much, and you are less inclined to choose unhealthy food because your diet is balanced.

- Is flexible, in that it changes according to your needs; you seek to eat nutritious food at home, at work and on the go.

- Is not rigid; you feel free to splurge once in a while because your diet is consistently wholesome and nourishing.

Simple Recipes and Strategies for a Better You

Eating and living well begins with adopting simple, wholesome food as the foundation of your diet. The approach that I recommend is to rotate a variety of vegetables, fruits, whole grains and high-quality proteins in a weekly meal plan that allows you to create endless combinations. This plan can fit any routine or health concern. By incorporating more of the foods highlighted in this book into your diet, you will simultaneously crowd out the less healthy choices. I have witnessed time and again that when my clients add more nutrient-dense food to their diets, a new level of wellness emerges.

Achieving success also requires cultivating habits that will support your intention to make positive change. This includes paying attention to how much you eat, when you eat, how you eat and how you feel after you eat. This cookbook provides recipes, strategies and practical advice to create a recipe for a healthy life.

I've Got a Recipe for a Healthy Life

How to Use This Book

LET'S GET COOKIN'

The intention of this cookbook is to empower you to expand your diet and cooking repertoire to include more **vegetables, fruits, whole grains, and high-quality proteins and fats.** The recipes should be considered templates for learning easy and fast preparation techniques, and are designed with customization in mind, for you to alter according to your tastes and nutritional needs. Ultimately, you will not need to remember a lot of recipes. Rather, this book provides basic skills training that will enable you to make the individual components of an endless variety of dishes that may be made from scratch or from leftovers.

The makeup of your optimal diet should be comprised of elements that fit your lifestyle and physical needs. For example, your schedule may require you to combine leftover food to take to work for lunch, or to take healthy snack food with you on the go. Most importantly, your food has to "work for you." When helping my clients, determining which foods can help to strengthen or weaken their individual bodies is part of the discovery process. You can start to do this evaluation on your own on a daily basis by paying attention to how particular foods impact how you feel and function, after a meal or even the next day.

Allergy-Free and Good for All

Many of the recipes included in this book are purposely gluten free so that a greater number of people can enjoy them, and because **they are delicious and nutritious.** In addition, gluten-free grains add color, texture and flexibility to your diet. I offer substitutions throughout the book for those looking to exclude dairy from their diets as well. Over the years, my experience has taught me that a lot of people are allergic or sensitive to gluten and/or dairy ingredients, which are causing or worsening many of their complaints. Could this be your concern? Information to help you to assess gluten intolerance is also provided in the coming pages.

Putting it All Together

While each of us requires a unique mix of vegetables, fruits, carbohydrates, fats and proteins for optimum health, most people would function best and may reach their self-improvement goals with this general strategy:

- Maintain a cumulative daily proportion of ⅓ **protein** (lean meats, nuts, seeds, beans including baby soybeans called edamame, and tofu); ⅓ **vegetables** (including 1-2 pieces of fruit); and ⅓ **carbohydrates** (whole grains, potatoes, corn, crackers, breads, chips, etc.), in addition to **healthy fats.**

- Enjoy healthy fats found naturally in nuts, seeds, beans (and hummus), avocados (and guacamole), as well as extra virgin olive oil, coconut oil and butter.

- Fill your lunch and dinner plates with ½ vegetables for weight loss or weight control.

- Don't skip breakfast. Eat protein with carbohydrates in the morning to jumpstart your day.

- For lunch, eat a mix of proteins, vegetables, and some carbohydrates—but not so much

that you become sleepy or tired a few hours later.

- For dinner, eat a balance of all three food groups.

- Choose snacks that contain fiber, protein, healthy fats and/or vegetables or fruits, being careful to limit your intake of added sugar.

- Keep sugary food, sweet drinks and alcohol to a minimum.

- Make water your preferred beverage.

Make it Your Own

My hope is that you will make these recipes your own, adding whatever spices and ingredient combinations you like. Try the suggested variations to fine-tune the recipes and to keep it interesting. The idea is to develop a weekly routine of cooking the basics and then supplement or change it as you go along. Using this book as a guide, you will acquire a new set of habits. You will become mindful of the need to slow down your eating, you will learn to balance your plate, and you will remember to carry nutrient-dense snacks with you, just to name a few healthy habits. This regimen and outlook will gradually become your "new normal."

The Surprise Ending

After incorporating a variety of nutrient-dense foods and establishing new habits into your life, you may notice that an unexpected gift has emerged. Your energy, digestion and sleep may improve, you may lose weight, your hair and skin may look noticeably improved, aches and pains may decrease, and you may feel stronger overall. When you start to feel better and more in control of your health, there is a ripple effect: you may be motivated to make positive change in other areas of your life as well. **Ultimately, the diet and the related habits that you create will support and sustain each other.** Enjoy the journey.

WHAT IS A RECIPE FOR A HEALTHY LIFE?

Yield:

A diet and lifestyle that support a strong foundation of health and happiness.

Ingredients:

*Whole Foods—*A healthy diet must contain mostly food that is whole, meaning the way nature made it, unprocessed and recognizable. It is no coincidence that all of your vital nutrients can be acquired by consuming the full color spectrum of vegetables, fruits, beans and grains. These are the foods that are most often lacking in people's diets. In life, no one wears the same outfit every day, so why should your food always be the same? You need a large, varied selection to truly thrive.

A "helping" of topics that include smart food shopping, meal planning, food portioning and proportions, gluten intolerance, and snacking away from home are included in each chapter for your reading consumption.

VARIATIONS: MIX IN "SPICES"

These are the ingredients **that give your life meaning:**
- regular exercise and movement
- meaningful work and connection to community
- time to explore spirituality or practice religious rituals
- nurturing relationships with family and friends
- an attitude of gratitude

When your life is filled with these "spices," you are less likely to use food to compensate for boredom, stress, or unhappiness. When you feel well from the inside out, you may see your world as full of opportunity and you are able to function with improved clarity and optimism.

71 FINAL THOUGHTS

CHAPTER ONE: LEAFY GREENS

"I'm strong to the finich, 'cause I eats me spinach, I'm Popeye the Sailor Man! (toot, toot)"
–Popeye (from the theme song)

Any healthy diet should include a frequent dose of leafy green energy in the form of *cooked greens* such as **kale, collards, baby bok choy, chard and spinach;** or *raw greens* such as **spinach, romaine, red and green lettuces, arugula, mesclun and baby bok choy.** This is what your body craves: food that lifts your spirits and mood, as well as your physical body, as the fiber moves digested food out of your system. If you are not accustomed to the depth of bitterness in this category, it is possible to cultivate a liking or even a preference for greens when you cook them in various ways. Keep an open mind and you will be richly rewarded.

Leafy greens are so powerful. Your bones absorb the calcium and magnesium that are found in abundance. Your tissues and organs soak up the iron, phosphorous, zinc, potassium, and vitamins A, C, E and K. Greens purify the blood, improve circulation, build intestinal flora and help to crowd out unhealthy food choices, because they satisfy your appetite at the deepest level.

Leafy greens can fit into any meal plan. Put leftover cooked greens in omelets, or throw them into a stir-fry at lunch or dinner. Layer them in sandwiches either cooked or raw. Leafy greens make a great addition to soups, sauces, pastas, casseroles, side dishes and of course, salads. Once you start including greens as a staple in your diet, you will enjoy finding new ways to prepare them every week.

RECIPES

TAKE STOCK OF YOUR KITCHEN

The kitchen is a place that should nourish you and your family. It should support your intention to be in control of how you take care of yourself. It's hard to commit to healthy eating with insufficient supplies. A kitchen stocked with high-quality whole foods sets you up to stay on track with good eating habits, and to be less dependent on eating out. If you are serious about improving your diet and health, the way to begin is to take stock, and restock your food supplies.

Take Stock

The process begins with reading labels. This will increase your awareness and buying power by knowing what you are actually consuming. A discriminating consumer, who consistently purchases food that is less processed and made with wholesome ingredients, is casting a vote for better products—and protecting his or her health as well.

What to Look for and Consider Removing

- When you look at a package label and see five or more ingredients and words you cannot pronounce, this is a sign that chemicals have been added to extend the shelf life of the product or to artificially enhance it in some way. Less is more in this context.

- Beware of products with hydrogenated oils, high fructose corn syrup, carrageenan, aspartame, sucralose and artificial colors, which are unhealthy and provide no positive value.

- The amount of sugar is one line to always read on the Nutrition Facts label. Although it includes both natural sugars (such as the fructose found in fruit or the lactose in milk) and added sugars, it provides a relative measure. Remember these equivalents: 4 grams of sugar = 1 teaspoon or one sugar packet; 12 grams of sugar = 1 tablespoon.

- Calories alone do not tell the whole story; it's the quality of the ingredients that matters.

- Beware of packages with cartoon characters and nutrition claims intended to appeal to young consumers in particular. The hype of packaged food is often disproportionate to its actual benefit, compared to the products that boast nothing—such as fruit-flavored roll-ups versus fresh apples.

- Discard any product that has passed its expiration date, or that looks or smells questionable.

Restock

On the following pages you will find a list of all of the ingredients and products that are used in this cookbook, plus some extras that will comprise a well-stocked kitchen. This is not to suggest that you would store all of these items at one time. Rather, it's a checklist that showcases the range and type of products that I keep in my own pantry, for you to consider. Brand names are noted when I recommend a specific allergen-free alternative.

Please note, I have included some canned goods and packaged products because I am not advocating that every food that you consume be made from scratch. It is realistic to expect that you may choose to purchase a container of vegetable broth, canned tomatoes, or precooked frozen brown rice for convenience. Within a product category, you could decide if you prefer dark chocolate chips made with milk and soy ingredients, or an allergen-free version made without either of those. Likewise, you might prefer red wine vinegar over balsamic, or brown rice pasta over whole wheat pasta. Experiment with product varieties. Enjoy the discovery.

A WELL-STOCKED KITCHEN

(and all of the ingredients used in this cookbook)

Whole Grain Products

black rice
brown rice
kasha buckwheat
millet
pearled barley
polenta
quinoa
rolled oats
instant plain oatmeal packets
wraps, pasta and soft tortillas
plain dry cereal

Beans

black
butter
cannellini
garbanzo
kidney
navy
pinto
red
white
dry split lentils

Prepared Soups

chili
lentil
chicken broth
vegetable broth

Snacks

KIND bars
nut butters
Wholly Guacamole
hummus
organic popcorn
100% whole grain crackers
tortilla chips
plain rice cakes

Herbs & Spices

allspice
black pepper
cardamom
cayenne
chili powder
chives
cilantro
cinnamon
cumin
curry powder
dill
garlic powder
ginger powder
Italian spice blend
onion powder
paprika/smoked paprika
parsley
pumpkin pie spice
red pepper flakes
rosemary
sea salt
turmeric

Baking Ingredients

agave syrup
pure maple syrup
honey
light brown sugar
baking powder
baking soda
canned 100% pure pumpkin
unsweetened cocoa powder
Enjoy Life or Chocolate Dream
chocolate chips
pure vanilla extract
Lundberg brown rice syrup
unsweetened shredded coconut
70-80% dark chocolate
raisins
dried berries
almonds
pine nuts
walnuts
peanuts
pecans
sunflower seeds
sesame seeds
pumpkin seeds
chia seeds
xanthan gum
unbleached all-purpose flour
whole wheat pastry flour
gluten-free flour
confectioners sugar

Condiments & Flavorings

soy sauce or San-J gluten-free tamari
Annie's salad dressing

yellow mustard
ketchup
various vinegars
white wine
tomato sauce
canned diced tomatoes
tomato paste
onions
garlic
ginger

———————

Vegetables

kale
collard greens
spinach
chard
lettuce
mixed baby greens
baby bok choy
broccoli
cauliflower
green beans
avocado
carrots
snow peas
cabbage
beets
parsnips
radishes
scallions
corn
zucchini
asparagus
bell peppers
tomatoes
celery
Brussels sprouts
Portobello mushrooms
white mushrooms
Mann's or Trader Joe's broccoli slaw
Yukon gold potatoes
fingerling potatoes
white potatoes

new potatoes
red potatoes
blue potatoes
orange sweet potatoes
yellow flesh yams
acorn squash
butternut squash
spaghetti squash

———————

Fruit

apples
pears
berries
melon
peaches
nectarines
clementines
pineapple
papaya
kiwi
mango
lemons
limes
pitted dates
bananas
oranges/juice
pomegranate

———————

Fats & Oils

extra virgin olive oil
olive oil
coconut oil
toasted sesame oil
tahini
canola oil
butter
Earth Balance coconut spread
mayonnaise
Vegenaise egg-free mayo

Protein

various fish
seafood
edamame
tofu
tempeh
beef
chicken
turkey
veggie burgers
organic eggs
organic chicken sausage

———————

Organic Dairy

milk
cottage cheese
plain unsweetened yogurt
goat cheese
feta
parmesan

———————

Dairy Alternatives

Earth Balance coconut spread
coconut, soy or almond yogurt
Daiya cheese
coconut, soy, rice or almond milk
So Delicious coconut milk beverage

———————

Miscellaneous

vinyl disposable gloves
baking spray with flour
pan spray

If you follow a gluten-free or allergen-free diet, read package labels and/or consult a trained professional to educate you to select products accordingly.

COLLARDS WITH MUSHROOMS AND ONIONS

Collard greens are hearty and satisfying prepared with just salt and olive oil. To keep it inviting, experiment with including other vegetables to add colors and flavors, and toppings to finish the dish.

Yield: 4 servings

8 oz. white or brown mushrooms
1 onion
1 large bunch collard greens
2 teaspoons extra virgin olive oil
Salt to taste

―――――――――

―――――――――

Instructions

1. Lightly rinse dirt off mushrooms and pat dry with a paper towel. Remove and discard stems. Slice mushroom caps and set aside.
2. Slice onion and set aside.
3. Rinse collard greens under running water. Remove stems and make a pile of the leaves.
4. Roll the leaves into a cigar shape and cut uniformly across the roll to create ribbons, also called chiffonade.
5. Place the cut leaves into a large skillet or saucepan with 1-2 cups of water. Simmer covered until leaves have turned bright green, or until tender. Drain and set aside.
6. Meanwhile, in a separate skillet, sauté onions in the oil for 3 minutes. Add mushrooms and continue to cook for another 2 minutes or until all of the mushroom liquid is gone. Pour mushroom and onion mixture on top of the collard greens, salt to taste and toss gently. Serve immediately.

Variations

- Drizzle 1 tablespoon of olive oil on cooked collard greens, salt to taste and sprinkle ¼ cup sunflower seeds, pumpkin seeds or chopped nuts on top.
- Sauté chopped red bell peppers, carrots or purple cabbage and combine with the cooked collard greens. Sauté until heated through to add visual contrast and a crunchy texture.
- Cut up precooked chicken or fish into bite-sized pieces and sauté until heated through in the same pan with the mushrooms and onions. Combine with the collard greens.
- Cut raw or cooked collard greens into bite-sized pieces and add to leftover soup. Simmer for 5 minutes or until leaves are tender and hot.

COLORFUL KALE

There are many ways to keep kale appealing and satisfying with its ability to complement any dish or ingredient. Sautéed broccoli slaw adds crunchy texture and color to the kale.

Yield: 4 servings

———————

Instructions

1. Detach the rinsed kale leaves from the stalks by hand or with a knife and discard the stalks. Set kale aside.
2. In a large skillet, heat oil over medium-high heat. Add the broccoli slaw or shredded vegetables and cook until softened, 1-2 minutes.
3. Add kale and 1 cup of water to the skillet. Cover and cook for 3-5 minutes until greens are tender and bright green. Drain any remaining water. Toss the vegetables so that the slaw is mixed into the kale, and serve.

1 bunch kale
1 tablespoon extra virgin olive oil
1 cup *Mann's* or *Trader Joe's* broccoli
        slaw (or any pre-shredded carrots
        or cabbage)
Salt to taste

———————

Variations

- Combine cooked kale with an equal or smaller amount of cooked pasta or whole grains.
- Replace the kale with collard greens, spinach or Swiss chard, and adjust cooking time of the greens until they are tender.
- Sauté onions and/or a few garlic cloves instead of the slaw or shredded vegetables.
- Serve with fish or meat and whole grains, or add precooked chicken or turkey, cut into small pieces, to the skillet and heat through for an additional 1-2 minutes.

WARM BEANS AND MIXED GREENS

Make this savory, warm salad dressing and add it to your favorite salad greens. It's so simple and yet so... gourmet!

Yield: 4 servings

---

14 oz. bag of mixed greens (or 2 5-8 oz. bags of spinach, romaine, mixed baby greens or butter lettuce)
1 cup shredded carrots
1 tablespoon extra virgin olive oil
1 small red onion, thinly sliced
1 15 oz. can garbanzo beans, rinsed and drained
1 teaspoon ground cumin

Dressing:
2 tablespoons lemon juice
2 teaspoons honey or agave syrup
2 tablespoons extra virgin olive oil
2 tablespoons soy sauce or gluten-free tamari
2 tablespoons water

Instructions

1. Cut salad greens if needed, or remove from bag(s) and combine with carrots in a large bowl.
2. In a small bowl, whisk together the lemon juice, sweetener, olive oil, soy sauce and water in a small bowl. Set dressing aside.
3. Heat 1 tablespoon olive oil in a medium skillet over medium-high heat. Sauté onion for 3 minutes.
4. Add beans and cumin and continue to cook for 1 minute.
5. Add the dressing, reduce the heat to low and simmer for 2-3 minutes.
6. Pour warm bean mixture over greens and serve.

Variations

- Try other kinds of beans or substitute with precooked chicken or fish cut into bite-sized pieces.

CHARD AND ONIONS WITH SPAGHETTI SQUASH

Yield: 2 servings

————————

1 spaghetti squash
1 bunch Swiss chard
1 small onion
1 tablespoon extra virgin olive oil
¼ cup water
Butter or olive oil (optional)
Garlic powder to taste (optional)
Salt to taste (optional)

Instructions

1. Preheat oven to 375°F.
2. Place entire squash in a baking pan, piercing the skin a few times like a potato. Bake for 20 minutes or until the skin has softened. Remove from the oven and cut in half lengthwise. Remove seeds and return to pan, cut side down. Bake 25 minutes longer, or until a knife easily pierces the flesh. Remove from oven and set aside.
3. Wash the chard. Cut out the stalks and discard them. Make a pile of the leaves and coarsely chop them. Rinse the chopped leaves in a large colander and set aside.
4. Rough chop the onion into small pieces.
5. Heat oil in a large skillet over medium heat. Add the onions and sauté for 3 minutes or until they look translucent.
6. Add the chard and water. Cover and simmer

Chard is similar to spinach in that it has a mild taste and cooks quickly. Swiss chard has glossy dark green leaves with a white stalk. Red chard has a red stalk and red veining in the leaves. Rainbow chard has five stalk and vein colors: yellow, orange, white, red and pink. If the stalks are included in a recipe, they are best separated from the leaves and cut into smaller pieces before cooking in order to cook as quickly as the leaves. Like other leafy greens, chard complements any grain or winter squash.

————————

Variations

- If any squash remains, reheat later for a snack and add a handful of chopped nuts, a sprinkle of cinnamon, and a bit of butter or olive oil and salt to taste. Tomato sauce would also complement the squash, as would a sprinkling of pumpkin or sunflower seeds.
- Leftover chard may be reheated as is, added to a stir-fry or soup, or combined with a cooked grain or pasta.

————————

for 1-2 minutes or until the leaves are wilted. Turn off heat and let the covered pan sit.
7. Using a fork, scoop out the spaghetti-like strands of squash and place in a large bowl. Add butter or oil and a dash of garlic powder or salt if you are using them, and toss to combine.
8. Serve a ½-¾ cup mound of squash on each plate, and top with an equally-sized portion of the cooked chard.

BABY BOK CHOY SALAD WITH ASIAN DRESSING

Baby bok choy has a mild taste with a surprise ending of gentle spiciness that adds character to all its variations, whether eaten raw or cooked.

Yield: 4-6 servings

————

Instructions

1. Add the garlic, orange juice, olive oil, sesame oil and soy sauce to a bowl and whisk to combine.
2. In a large bowl, combine the baby bok choy, cabbage and carrots, and toss with the dressing. Sprinkle with sesame or sunflower seeds and serve immediately. Any remaining dressing may be stored in the refrigerator for up to 4 days.

————

More grocery stores now carry baby bok choy, but they can always be found at Asian markets.

6 baby bok choy, finely chopped with the root end removed
1 cup coarsely shredded purple cabbage
½ cup shredded carrots
Sesame or sunflower seeds (optional)

Dressing:
2 cloves garlic, minced or pressed
3 tablespoons orange juice
2 tablespoons extra virgin olive oil
1 tablespoon toasted sesame oil
1 tablespoon soy sauce or gluten-free tamari

————

Variations

- Replace the orange juice with 2 tablespoons of flavored vinegar.
- Add bite-sized pieces of chicken or fish to a serving bowl and toss with the other ingredients.

SPINACH WITH FRIED PASTA

My favorite way to bring leftover pasta back to life is to gently sauté it with freshly cooked or reheated vegetables. Fried pasta becomes both soft in some spots and crunchy in others, a texture combination that's not experienced when it's initially prepared. In this recipe, the spinach cooks simultaneously with the reheated pasta and becomes a meal in just five minutes.

Yield: 4 servings

2 tablespoons extra virgin olive oil
2-3 cups leftover whole wheat or gluten-free pasta
6 oz. bag fresh baby spinach
¼ cup grated parmesan or crumbled goat cheese

Instructions

1. Heat oil in a large nonstick skillet on medium heat for a minute. Add the pasta to the pan and separate it with a spoon as it warms, until all of the pieces have contact with the pan. Cover the skillet for 2 minutes and continue to cook, then flip the pasta over and cook for 2 more minutes to get it crispy on both sides.

2. Add spinach to the skillet and cook covered for 2 minutes, or until leaves are wilted.

3. Sprinkle cheese on top of the mixture and transfer to a serving bowl.

Variations

- Top pasta with nuts or seeds.
- Sauté any combination of onions, garlic, broccoli, cauliflower, peppers, mushrooms, bok choy, kale or chard, and add pasta to the skillet for the last 4 minutes of cooking.
- Add any kind of cooked meat, fish or beans to the skillet in place of or in addition to the vegetables at the end of cooking and heat through.

CHAPTER TWO: RAINBOW VEGETABLES

"Eat food. Not too much. Mostly plants." –Michael Pollan,
In Defense of Food: An Eater's Manifesto

Color Becomes You!

We need to eat vegetables several times each day in order to keep up with our bodies' need for water soluble vitamin C, and the B vitamins.[1] Since these vitamins cannot be produced by the body or stored for very long, they are called "essential nutrients," which is why US government guidelines recommend that adults consume at least 2 to 2½ cups daily.[2] We can survive with the minimum, but we cannot truly thrive without eating a generous helping on our plates.

Vegetables have the highest density of nutrients and the lowest number of calories compared to fats, proteins and grains, making it vital that they be well represented in everyone's diet. Moreover, each vegetable is unique, possessing its own combination of vitamins, minerals and fiber. It appears that nature has designed each vegetable so that it has a distinct color and shape. By consuming a variety of vegetables encompassing the entire color spectrum whenever possible, we contribute to protecting and enhancing our health.

RECIPES

DRINK TO YOUR HEALTH

Find a Way to Love Your Water and Keep it Nearby

The importance of consuming enough water cannot be overstated. The standard recommendation is to drink eight glasses of water per day in order to adequately support the function of your organs. If you are not drinking enough, you may experience **poor digestion, dry skin, headaches, bad breath and fatigue.** Furthermore, you need to pay extra attention to keeping your body hydrated in the winter when the indoor air is dry, in the summer when you sweat more, in dry climates, and at any time when you are exercising or otherwise exerting yourself. Even with this knowledge, it can still be challenging to drink enough water to satisfy your body's needs.

The key is to like the taste of the water you are drinking, and to feel confident that it is clean and healthy. Purified water tastes better, which may motivate you to drink more of it. Some people like purified bottled water with added minerals and electrolytes. Others prefer to use water filtering pitchers or other water filtration systems to provide clean tap water at home. Distilled water is never recommended for hydration because the trace minerals have been removed. This pure form of water actually acts against you, absorbing healthy electrolytes and other elements from your cells rather than hydrating the body. Sometimes people buy it by mistake or because it's cheaper, as it is located with the purified drinking water at the store. For those who like a bit of flavor added to their drinks, it's easy to add a squeeze of lemon or lime, or to mix in a little fruit juice to make it more palatable. Sparkling water or seltzer are also great options.

Six Guidelines for Filling up on Water

1. Drink a glass of water when you first wake up in the morning, when you are generally the most dehydrated.

2. If consuming eight glasses of water per day is not realistic, drink enough so that your urine is very light in color. On days that you are traveling or are exposed to a lot of germs, you should drink more.

3. Drink a glass of water if you feel sleepy or sluggish during the day, and are tempted to reach for coffee, soda or a sweet treat. Thirst can feel like hunger, so wait 15 minutes to see if a glass of water perks you up before consuming something else.

4. Herbal teas and vegetable juices count toward your water goals and have the added benefit of providing vitamins and minerals. Soda, coffee and alcohol do not count toward daily fluid intake because they dehydrate your body and can cause nutrient loss. Check the nutrition labels on bottled water to determine if other ingredients have been added, such as sugar or artificial sweeteners and colors.

5. Keep water available wherever you are, i.e. your car, desk and nightstand, so that you won't forget to sip throughout the day. Avoid keeping plastic bottles of water in a hot car so that the hazardous chemicals found in plastic do not leach into the water.

6. Foods with high fluid content, such as vegetables, fruits and cooked grains, also count toward your daily water intake and can help to eliminate waste from your body. The recipes in this cookbook will help you to increase the quantity of water-dense foods in your diet.

MEDITERRANEAN MEDLEY

The olive oil and spices in this dish make it one of my favorites. Almost any vegetable combination can fit into this enticing mix of textures and colors.

Yield: 8 servings

Instructions

1. Preheat oven to 375°F.
2. Chop the carrots into 1-inch pieces and the broccoli, cauliflower and zucchini into 2-inch pieces. Set aside.
3. Slice or chop the garlic, and chop the onions into small chunks.
4. If you have a pitcher-style measuring cup, measure the olive oil into it and add the lemon juice. If not, add both to a small bowl. Combine with the turmeric, paprika, cumin, ginger and salt, using a whisk.
5. Place all of the vegetables and beans in a large roasting pan.
6. Bake uncovered for 45-60 minutes or until all of the vegetables are well cooked, or fork tender.

2 carrots
1 large crown broccoli
1 small cauliflower
2 zucchini
5 cloves garlic
2 onions
½ cup grape tomatoes
1 15 oz. can garbanzo beans, rinsed

Dressing:
¾ cup extra virgin olive oil
Juice of ½ lemon
1 teaspoon turmeric
2 teaspoons paprika
1½ teaspoons cumin
½ teaspoon powdered ginger
1 teaspoon salt

Variations

• Add or substitute with Brussels sprouts cut in half or quartered; green bell peppers cut into long strips; or yams, parsnips, or butternut squash cut into 2-inch pieces.

ROASTED ROOT VEGETABLES

A healthy and enjoyable way to reduce sugar cravings and potentially lose weight is to add naturally sweet foods like root vegetables to your diet, to replace those made with added sweeteners.

Yield: 8 servings

---

4 medium beets
2 large carrots
2 parsnips
2 red or yellow onions
9 oz. Brussels sprouts
10 cloves garlic
2 tablespoons extra virgin olive oil
1 tablespoon fresh rosemary, finely chopped with stems removed (optional)
Salt to taste

Instructions

1. Preheat oven to 425°F.
2. Peel beets, carrots, parsnips and onions, and chop into 2-inch pieces.
3. Discard bottoms of Brussels sprouts and cut in half. Peel the garlic.
4. Lightly coat all of the vegetables with oil, rosemary and salt in a large roasting pan or baking dish.
5. Bake uncovered for 25-30 minutes or until a knife can pierce easily through each type of vegetable.

Variations

- Add or substitute additional root or starchy vegetables such as turnips, winter squash like butternut and acorn, sweet potatoes, yams or corn.

WHIPPED CAULIFLOWER AND POTATOES

Cauliflower easily transitions to a whipped, mashed texture by itself or with a small amount of potato added. Depending on the potato, it can be made either sweet or savory. This synergistic combination enhances the flavors of both the cauliflower and the potato.

Yield: 4-6 servings

---

2 Yukon gold potatoes or any type of sweet potato/yam
1 cauliflower
2 tablespoons olive oil or butter
½ teaspoon fresh or ¼ teaspoon dried dill
Salt and black pepper to taste

Instructions

1. Remove the skin if using yams or sweet potatoes, but keep the skin on and scrub it well if you are using Yukon gold potatoes. Cut up the cauliflower and potatoes into small pieces and place in a steamer.
2. Steam for 5-8 minutes or until the cauliflower and potatoes are easily pierced with a knife.
3. Place the vegetables in a food processor and run until the mixture is smooth, like mashed potatoes. Add oil or butter, dill, and salt and pepper to taste.
4. If the mixture cooled significantly during blending, place in a baking dish, reheat for 5-10 minutes in a 350°F oven, and serve hot.

Variations

- Substitute potatoes with winter squash.
- Double the amount of cauliflower and whip by itself.
- Serve green or leafy green vegetables such as sautéed kale, bok choy or broccoli with this dish to provide a bright contrast in color as well as a nutritional boost.

GARLIC ASPARAGUS AND PORTOBELLOS

In this recipe asparagus adds colorful crunch, the Portobellos are soft and chewy, and the garlic adds a spicy kick.

Yield: 2-4 servings

1 lb. fresh asparagus
5-6 oz. Portobello mushrooms
3-4 cloves garlic, minced
2 tablespoons extra virgin olive oil
½ teaspoon salt

Instructions

1. Preheat oven to 400°F.
2. Cut off the woody ends of the asparagus and then divide each stalk into thirds or bite-sized pieces. Set aside in a bowl.
3. Slice the mushrooms into thin strips and add to the bowl along with the minced garlic.
4. Pour olive oil and salt into the bowl. Stir to combine until the vegetables are evenly coated.
5. Roast for 15-20 minutes or until the vegetables are browned, tossing once about halfway through cooking. Serve immediately.

Variations

- Any size or kind of mushrooms will work here.
- This dish pairs nicely with brown rice, either mixed in or served as a separate side dish.
- Combine leftovers with eggs to make an omelet.

NOT-YOUR-CHILDHOOD BRUSSELS SPROUTS

People either love or hate Brussels sprouts. This is my effort to tempt the most resistant foes to give this wonderful winter vegetable another try. By browning the Brussels sprouts, they become soft, caramelized and less bitter. The other vegetables add color and sweetness to this wholesome dish.

Yield: 4 servings

---

9 oz. Brussels sprouts (or 9 oz. package of
      ***Trader Joe's* shredded Brussels sprouts)**
¼ small purple cabbage
1 cup shredded carrots
2 tablespoons olive oil or coconut oil
Salt to taste
1 tablespoon toasted sesame oil

Instructions

1. Shred Brussels sprouts and cabbage into thin pieces. Cut up carrots as well, if they are not pre-shredded.
2. Drizzle olive or coconut oil into a large skillet and preheat for one minute. Place carrots, Brussels sprouts and cabbage in the pan and cook covered over medium heat for approximately 8 minutes, tossing gently every couple of minutes.
3. When the vegetables are soft and lightly browned, salt to taste, drizzle with sesame oil and toss to coat. Serve immediately.

Variations

- Green cabbage or cauliflower and/or onions also work here in place of the purple cabbage and carrots.
- This dish can also be eaten cold, and it is delicious topped with chopped peanuts or sesame seeds.

ROASTED FRENCH-CUT GREEN BEANS

French-cut green beans are easy to prepare and can be jazzed up with a sprinkling of almonds or seeds to create a hearty, crunchy side dish.

Yield: 2-4 servings

───────────

12 oz. package of fresh French-cut green beans
¼ cup slivered almonds
1½ tablespoons extra virgin olive oil
Salt to taste

Instructions

1. Preheat oven to 375°F.
2. Place green beans and almonds in a bowl and toss with the olive oil and salt to coat.
3. Arrange green beans on a baking sheet in a single layer.
4. Roast in the oven for 15-20 minutes or until the green beans are browned but still crunchy.

───────────

Variations

- In place of the almonds, sunflower, pumpkin or sesame seeds can provide the same texture and appetizing presentation.

BROCCOLI AND POTATO SLAW

This colorful side dish is a cross between potato salad and coleslaw, to be eaten warm or cold. Whether the potatoes are leftover or roasted for this purpose, they combine perfectly with any shredded and sautéed vegetable to make a nourishing and filling side dish or snack.

Yield: 2-4 servings

_____

1 lb. blue potatoes (or a mix of small colorful/fingerling potatoes)
12 oz. package *Mann's* or *Trader Joe's* broccoli slaw
3 tablespoons extra virgin olive oil, divided
Salt

Dressing:
1 tablespoon lemon juice
1 tablespoon mustard
2 teaspoons agave syrup
½ teaspoon dried dill
½ teaspoon salt

Instructions

1. Preheat oven to 400°F.
2. Wash the potatoes and pat dry. Cut potatoes into bite-sized pieces.
3. Combine potatoes, salt and 2 tablespoons olive oil in a bowl and toss to coat.
4. Spread the potatoes in a single layer on a heavy baking sheet and bake uncovered for about 15 minutes, or until the potatoes are fork tender and lightly browned. Gently toss the potatoes about halfway through cooking.
5. Remove potatoes from the oven and let cool on the tray.
6. In the meantime, drizzle 1 tablespoon of oil into a large skillet and heat briefly on medium heat before placing the precut slaw in the pan. Cover and cook for 3-5 minutes, stirring occasionally with tongs. When the vegetables are bright but wilted and lightly browned in some places, remove pan from heat and cool uncovered.
7. To make the dressing, combine the lemon juice, mustard, agave, dill and salt in a small bowl. Mix cooled potatoes and slaw together in a large serving bowl and toss to coat with the dressing. Serve immediately if eating it warm, or refrigerate and eat it cold later.

_____

Variations

- Shred a total of 5 cups of carrots and purple or green cabbage, and/or add small pieces of broccoli to sauté, then mix in with the potatoes.
- Use precooked vegetables that have been cut into small pieces to stand in for the suggestions above.
- Reheat entire mixture in a skillet and add scrambled eggs for a hearty breakfast.
- Add tuna or shredded chicken plus a few teaspoons of mayonnaise to make a quick and delicious snack or lunch.

BARLEY WITH EDAMAME AND SPINACH PESTO, p. 29

CHAPTER THREE: HEARTY WHOLE GRAINS

"Whole-grain pasta, breads and cereals are valuable foods, but
whole grains in their simplicity and wholeness are healing."
–Joanne Saltzman, *Amazing Grains*

Whole grains are grains that have not been processed and refined. They contain all of the major nutrient groups and contribute to what the body requires every day: carbohydrates, proteins, fats, fiber, B-complex vitamins, vitamin E, iron and minerals.

Each kind of whole grain has its own texture, color, taste and nutritional strength. In cooking, they can be used interchangeably.

The whole grains that I highlight in this book are brown and black rice, quinoa, oats, millet, barley, kasha buckwheat and polenta (corn). The grains in the following recipes can be swapped out with any other grain; see the Whole Grains Cooking Chart (p. 24) for guidance.

I have intentionally omitted any recipes that contain wheat (even 100% whole wheat) because our western diet is disproportionately comprised of wheat in our breads and other baked goods, pasta, soups and elsewhere. Furthermore, wheat (and its gluten protein) is one of the foods most commonly associated with food allergies and sensitivities. My goal is to help you to reduce the quantity of wheat products, and incorporate more variety and creativity using alternative whole grains, in your diet.

RECIPES

GLUTEN FREE: A "FAD" DIET WORTH CONSIDERING

The gluten-free diet has attracted a lot of media attention as the answer to many problems including weight gain, digestive issues and weakness, with more than a few athletes and movie stars endorsing its various benefits. Is this a fad, or a prescription for the multitudes? Some in the medical community and various other naysayers criticize the trend as a fad that is attracting too many people who are randomly seeking a solution to their diet or health woes.

Based on my personal and professional experience, this is the one diet that's actually worth considering, along with gluten intolerance testing for those who have unresolved chronic health concerns. While gluten is not a problem for the majority of the populace, according to Dr. David Perlmutter, up to 40% of the population may be getting sick from it.[3] The research on gluten-related disorders is exploding with proof that gluten can trigger an inflammatory response anywhere in the body, and can cause or worsen many autoimmune diseases and health problems.

What is Gluten?

Gluten is the generic name for certain types of proteins contained in wheat, barley and rye, and also found in oats because of cross-contamination through harvesting or processing. When someone who cannot tolerate gluten eats foods containing that substance, it creates an immune reaction that causes damage to the small intestine, and an inflammatory response that can travel beyond the gut. Even small amounts of gluten in foods can damage the small intestine and **trigger many sorts of health problems** *even if one doesn't appear to have symptoms.*

Gluten-related disorder is a new term used to describe all conditions related to gluten allergy or intolerance. Its subsets include celiac disease (CD) and non-celiac gluten sensitivity (NCGS), which are genetic predispositions affecting people of all ages and ethnicities.[4] People with CD have flattened villi in their small intestines after repeated exposure to gluten, whereas people with NCGS do not have this autoimmune response. People with both types of conditions require a gluten-free diet, and can experience almost all of the same symptoms throughout the body.

Where is Gluten?

We generally consume more gluten than we realize, since a lot of it is hidden and unnoticeable. Consider this:

- Food manufacturers add gluten to wheat flours to give them more binding power. This is why our breads and bagels are so chewy and tasty.

- Gluten is a common additive in many packaged, bottled and canned foods. It enhances the texture by binding, thickening or coating the food.

- Today's bioengineers cultivate grains with high amounts of gluten in order to improve the end product. It is estimated that wheat today contains almost 90% more gluten than it did 100 years ago![5]

- Wheat, barley and rye derivatives exist in foods where you might not expect to find them: soy sauce, salad dressings, processed meat, soups, candy, alcohol and flavored coffee, to name a few of the many thousands of such products.

All of the recipes in this cookbook are gluten free or can be converted accordingly. If you are not gluten intolerant, you are fortunate indeed. However, it is still unhealthy to eat a lot of the same foods every day because this creates an imbalance in your diet. We need variety to obtain all of the nutrients that nature has to offer, and that are available for humans to consume and enjoy, in adequate amounts.

Do You Have a Gluten-Related Disorder?

It is estimated that there are nearly 200 problems that someone who cannot tolerate gluten may experience (see the list below). A person with a gluten-related disorder may have none, one, or several of these conditions. This type of disorder is difficult to diagnose without testing because you may not be aware that you have symptoms, or that they are related to any one condition. It's also complicated because these problems can have other causes unrelated to gluten, they may be worsened by gluten, or they may be caused by gluten.

A <u>partial</u> list of problems or conditions caused or worsened by gluten in people with a gluten-related disorder:[6]

Digestive

Acid reflux
Bloating
Canker sores
Constipation
Diarrhea
Fructose intolerance
Irritable bowel syndrome
Lactose intolerance
Liver disease
Pancreatitis
Steatorrhea (fatty floating stools)

_____

Skin

Acne
Alopecia areata (hair loss)
Eczema
Dry skin
Psoriasis
Dark circles under eyes

Emotional

Anxiety
Irritability
Depression

_____

Physical Wellbeing

Fatigue
Difficulty losing or gaining weight
Poor endurance
Chronic fatigue
Failure to thrive
Short stature

_____

Mind/Neurological

Autism
ADHD
Mental fog
Insomnia/difficulty sleeping
Epilepsy

Musculoskeletal

Arthritis
Fibromyalgia
Muscle aches/joint pains
Osteopenia/osteoporosis
Respiratory
Wheezing
Chronic sinusitis
Asthma

_____

Women's Health

Irregular cycle
Infertility
Miscarriage
Headaches/migraines

_____

Miscellaneous

Anemia
Raynaud's disease (cold hands/feet)
Autoimmune disorders
Hashimoto's disease
Lupus (SLE)
Thyroiditis

While laboratories today can perform accurate testing for NCDS and NCGS,[7] one can also eliminate gluten completely from their diet for 30 days to assess whether it makes a difference. However, an elimination diet has to be 100% free of gluten in order to be certain of the outcome. Many people experience a detox, or malaise, when they initially remove gluten from their diet. Ultimately, if you feel better without gluten, then it is a good indication that this diet would serve you well. Please note that a laboratory test needs to detect antibodies from the gluten in order to be accurate. Therefore, if you truly eliminate gluten before testing, it may be too late to take a test.

WHOLE GRAINS COOKING CHART

Photocopy and attach to the inside of your cupboard

1 cup of dry grain	Grain to water ratio	For added flavor, try alternative liquids	Approximate cooking time
Brown rice	1:2	1/2 coconut milk + 1/2 water, rice milk, vegetable or chicken broth	45-50 minutes
Quinoa	1:2	vegetable or chicken broth or 1/2 tomato sauce + 1/2 water	15-20 minutes
Millet	1:3	1/2 coconut milk + 1/2 water	20 minutes
Buckwheat (kasha)	1:2	vegetable or chicken broth	20 minutes
Barley (pearled)	1:2	vegetable or chicken broth or 1/2 tomato sauce + 1/2 water	40-50 minutes
Oatmeal (rolled oats)	1:2-3	rice, soy or almond milk or 1/2 coconut milk + 1/2 water	10-15 minutes
Oats (steel cut/ Irish oats)	1:3-4	rice, soy or almond milk or 1/2 apple juice + 1/2 water	30 minutes

BASIC INSTRUCTIONS FOR COOKING GRAINS

One cup of dry grain yields approximately 3 cups cooked.

One cup of dry oats yields approximately 2½ cups cooked.

1.

There are two ways to wash grains. Measure the grains and place in an empty pot, fill with water and swish grains around to clean off dust and natural debris. Empty water from pot and refill with recommended amount of water or liquid for cooking. Or, place grains in a strainer to rinse before placing in pot and filling with water or other liquid for cooking.

2.

Bring water and grains to a boil (except for buckwheat/kasha–boil water first and then add grains).

3.

A pinch of sea salt may be added while cooking.

4.

Reduce heat to a simmer and cover pot for the recommended time. *Do not stir grains while cooking.* Check to see if grains are done by tilting pot to the side to see that no water remains.

MILLET AND VEGETABLE BLEND

Talk about multi-tasking: preparing this combination of grains and vegetables saves time and can be part of a satisfying meal!

Millet *may be recognized as yellow birdseed, even though it has been an important food staple in Africa for thousands of years. It is considered the easiest grain to digest and its texture can be fluffy or creamy, depending on the type and amount of cooking liquid that is used. This recipe creates a drier version of the dish but it could be made creamier with an extra ½ cup of liquid.*

Yield: 4 servings

1 cup millet
2½ cups water or vegetable broth
2½ cups mixed broccoli and cauliflower
    florets
1 tablespoon olive oil or butter
Salt to taste

Instructions

1. Place the millet in a fine mesh strainer and rinse under cool running water. Add millet and water or broth to a medium saucepan. Add vegetables, cover with a lid and bring contents to a boil.
2. Turn the heat to low and simmer for 20-30 minutes, never stirring but watching to see when the water has been completely absorbed. Millet will be done when water no longer runs out from the bottom when the pot is tilted to its side.
3. Add olive oil or butter and salt to taste. Stir to combine. Serve immediately.

Variations

- For a sweeter taste, use carrots, parsnips and/or beets in place of the broccoli and cauliflower. Remember to cut the root vegetables into a small dice, since they will take longer to cook than other vegetables.
- Add cooked millet to the protein on your plate or use it as the base of a stir-fry.

ORANGE QUINOA

By adding a flavorful liquid to cook the quinoa, it tastes like something new. This dish works with both vegetables and proteins, or it can be eaten as a delicious hot breakfast cereal.

__Quinoa__ (pronounced keen-wah) has been a staple in the diet of native South Americans for thousands of years. It is not technically a grain, but rather is the seed of a plant. Quinoa is touted as a super food because of its high protein content and energy-producing quality. Quinoa must be rinsed well after measuring and before cooking to remove the bitter, soapy-tasting saponins that coat the seeds.

1 cup quinoa
2 cups orange juice
¼ cup sliced almonds or chopped walnuts
Salt to taste

_____

Yield: 4-6 servings

_____

Instructions

1. Rinse the quinoa in a strainer or swish it around in a pot with water and then drain the water.
2. Place the rinsed quinoa and orange juice in a saucepan and heat on high until boiling.
3. Reduce heat, cover and simmer approximately 15-20 minutes. Do not stir.
4. Quinoa will be done when water no longer runs out from the bottom when the pot is tilted to its side.
5. Fold the nuts into the mixture, salt to taste, and place in a serving bowl.

Variations

- Any vegetable and protein combination, such as fish and kale or chicken and asparagus, complements this dish without overpowering its light texture and slightly sweet flavor.
- To make a hot breakfast cereal, measure ¾ cup of cold, cooked grain into a frying pan. Add a sprinkle of cinnamon, a handful of raisins, and ¼ cup of orange juice. Thinly slice half of a banana into the pan as well. Heat on low, stirring until the mixture is warmed up and the bananas have softened.

COCONUT MILLET

Coconut milk complements millet in both savory and sweet dishes. This basic recipe can be eaten as is, mixed into a stir-fry or refashioned as a hot breakfast cereal.

Yield: 4-6 servings

————————

1 cup millet
1½ cups water
1½ cups *So Delicious* boxed coconut milk beverage (coconut milk in a can is thicker
**   but also works)**
¼ cup unsweetened shredded coconut (optional)
1 tablespoon butter or non-dairy spread
Salt to taste

————————

Instructions

1. Rinse the millet in a fine mesh strainer under cool running water.
2. Place in a medium saucepan with the water, coconut milk, and shredded coconut. Bring to a boil. Then reduce the heat, cover and simmer for approximately 20 minutes. Do not stir.
3. Millet will be done when water no longer runs out from the bottom when the pot is tilted to its side. Stir in butter and salt, and transfer mixture to a serving bowl.

————————

Variations

- To make this recipe using brown or black rice instead of millet, add 1 cup rice + 1 cup water + 1 cup coconut milk to the pot. Bring to a boil and simmer for approximately 40 minutes, or until liquid is absorbed.
- To make a hot breakfast cereal, place ¾ cup cold, cooked millet or rice into a small skillet over medium heat + ⅓ cup milk or non-dairy substitute + a dash of cinnamon + a small handful of nuts and/or raisins. Cook until all of the milk is absorbed, stirring occasionally.

BARLEY WITH EDAMAME AND SPINACH PESTO

Pictured on p. 20

Pearled barley, *though partially processed to allow for faster cooking times than whole barley, provides protein, fat and minerals to dishes. It has a sturdy, chewy texture that blends well with vegetables and soups, or it can be served on its own as a simple side dish. To spice up and enliven this recipe, add this spinach pesto as a side sauce or mix into the barley before serving.*

Edamame (pronounced ed-a-mom-may) is high in protein and fiber, but unlike mature soybeans, these are easier to digest. Edamame can be purchased fresh or frozen, in the pod or shelled. They can be eaten as a snack or added to stir-frys and salads.

Yield: 4-6 servings

_____

1 cup pearled barley
2 cups water
1 tablespoon extra virgin olive oil
2 cups chopped cauliflower
1 cup shredded carrots
1 cup shelled fresh or precooked frozen
     edamame
Salt to taste
Garlic powder or your favorite spices
     (optional)

Pesto:
1-2 cloves garlic
½ cup extra virgin olive oil
3 tablespoons lemon juice
1 teaspoon paprika/smoked paprika
½ teaspoon cumin
½ teaspoon salt
1½ cups baby spinach, tightly packed
½ cup parsley, stems removed

Instructions

1. Rinse the barley well in a strainer and place in a pot with the water. Bring to a boil.
2. Reduce the heat, cover and simmer approximately 20 minutes. Do not stir. The barley is done when water no longer runs out from the bottom when the pot is tilted to its side.
3. If the edamame is frozen, follow the package instructions to boil it in water.
4. Heat a skillet coated with the oil over medium heat and sauté the cauliflower and carrots for 5 minutes. Mix in the boiled or precooked edamame and a dash of salt or your favorite spices, such as garlic powder or black pepper. Sauté for another 3-5 minutes.
5. While the barley and vegetables are cooling, make the spinach pesto. Chop the garlic by itself in the food processor. Then add the olive oil, lemon juice, paprika, cumin, salt, spinach and parsley, and process until well blended. Mix all or part of the pesto into the barley. Serve any pesto that remains on the side, or save to top leftovers.
6. When both the vegetables and barley are cooked, combine in a serving dish, or serve 1½ cups of the edamame mixture on top of ¾ cup of barley per serving.

_____

Variations

- Frozen corn can easily join the edamame for the last 2 minutes of cooking for more color and variety.
- Add chopped red or yellow bell peppers, broccoli or snow peas instead of the carrots and cauliflower. Choose your vegetables to create a colorful and textured presentation that will delight your eyes and your taste buds.
- For a gluten-free version, barley can easily be replaced with brown rice, quinoa or millet.

BROWN RICE PILAF

Brown, black and red rice *have intact bran layers and are considered whole grains, whereas white rice has been stripped of its bran and is not a whole grain. While brown rice takes longer to cook than white rice, the fiber and nutrients found in this versatile and always-satisfying dish are worth the wait.*

Plain brown rice is a staple in many diets, but once in a while it's nice to dress it up a little. You'll enjoy this flavorful pilaf made with a couple of added "accessories."

Yield: 4 servings

1 cup brown basmati rice
2 cups water or vegetable/chicken broth
½ teaspoon salt
1 medium onion
1 tablespoon chopped fresh parsley
¼ cup pine nuts or chopped walnuts
1 tablespoon extra virgin olive oil

Instructions

1. Rinse rice in a fine mesh strainer until the water runs clear.
2. Add the water or broth to a saucepan and bring to a boil. Add rice and salt, cover and reduce heat to low. Do not stir.
3. While the rice is cooking, dice the onion and chop the parsley and nuts if necessary.
4. Drizzle olive oil into a skillet and heat for a minute on medium heat. Add the onions and nuts and sauté for 5 minutes. Turn off heat and stir in parsley.
5. Rice will be done when water no longer runs out from the bottom when the pot is tilted to its side.
6. Add cooked rice to the skillet and stir to combine. Serve warm or cold.

Variations

- The type and quantity of mix-ins can vary according to your preferences. Broccoli florets, sliced or diced scallions, carrots, mushrooms or green bell peppers, as well as nuts or seeds, can make a unique pilaf. Paprika, garlic powder or your favorite spice can be added while the vegetables are being sautéed.

POLENTA WITH BOK CHOY

Polenta, *made from ground corn, provides a sweet boost of energy that is also comforting and filling. Rolls of precooked polenta can easily be found in the produce section of most grocery stores or on the shelf at Trader Joe's. It is easy to make and can be a nutritious part of any meal.*

I recommend that you prepare the whole package as suggested in this recipe, so that you may enjoy any leftovers at a future meal. Otherwise, when you purchase this precooked packaged type of polenta, you must refrigerate the remainder after opening it.

Yield: 4-6 servings

———————

1 pound precooked polenta
1 red bell pepper
4-6 baby bok choy
2 tablespoons + 1 teaspoon olive oil, divided
Italian spice blend (optional)
Salt to taste

Instructions

1. Cut polenta into ¼-inch slices. Drizzle 2 tablespoons olive oil into a large nonstick skillet and heat on medium-high for 1-2 minutes.
2. Place polenta in the pan and fry for 4-5 minutes on each side or until it turns a dark yellow. Add a dash of Italian seasoning if desired. Keep the polenta covered while cooking. (It may take two rounds of cooking if your skillet is not large enough to hold all of the slices at once).
3. Meanwhile, cut the pepper into matchsticks. Rinse the bok choy, cut off the bottom ends and discard. Chop, keeping the stalks and green leaves separate.
4. When the polenta is cooked, remove from the pan and set aside in a covered serving dish.
5. To the same pan, add 1 teaspoon of olive oil, the peppers, and the stalks of bok choy. Cook for 2-3 minutes, stirring occasionally. Add remaining greens to the pan and continue to cook covered for a minute, or until the greens are wilted.
6. Salt to taste. Pour the entire mixture on top of the polenta and serve hot. Leftovers can be eaten hot or cold.

———————

Variations

- Chard, spinach, diced vegetables or leftover cooked vegetables can easily fit into this recipe.
- Other spices that may complement this dish include garlic powder, onion powder, black pepper, cayenne pepper or any of your favorites.

QUINOA AVOCADO MEDLEY

Just as various leaves make a superb base for a green salad, quinoa can be the foundation of a vegetable grain salad. Cut vegetables into small pieces so as not to overwhelm the small, delicate grain. Warm, cooked grains can be shaped with a container such as a measuring cup for a unique presentation.

Yield: 6 servings

1 cup quinoa
2 cups water or vegetable/chicken broth
½ cup sliced carrots
1 cup diced yellow or orange bell peppers
1 cup diced zucchini
1 ripe avocado
Juice of one lemon
1 tablespoon + 2 teaspoons extra virgin
     olive oil, divided
1 ripe avocado
Salt to taste

Instructions

1. Rinse the quinoa thoroughly, either in a fine mesh strainer or in a pot, and drain.
2. Place quinoa in a medium pot with the water or broth. Bring to a boil, then reduce heat to low and simmer covered for about 15 minutes or until all of the liquid is absorbed. Do not stir.
3. Quinoa will be done when water no longer runs out from the bottom when the pot is tilted to its side. Place quinoa in a serving bowl.
4. While the quinoa is cooking, prepare the vegetables. Heat 1 tablespoon of oil in a large skillet over medium heat. Add the carrots and peppers and sauté for 3 minutes. Stir in the zucchini and cook for another 3 minutes. Remove pan from heat.
5. Peel and dice the avocado. Set aside.
6. In a small bowl, combine the lemon juice with 2 teaspoons of oil. Add the avocado and gently toss with the dressing.
7. Fold the cooked vegetables and avocado mixture into the quinoa.
8. Add salt to taste.
9. If you choose to, pack a 1-cup measuring cup with quinoa salad and flip over onto individual plates. Serve warm.

Variations

- Top individual servings with sliced avocado instead of including in the mixture. This is the better option if you are going to have leftovers, as diced avocado tossed with the dressing will turn brown.
- Add nuts or seeds to the grain salad.
- Other diced vegetables to swap in: broccoli, tomatoes, snow peas, cauliflower or green beans.
- Any grain can be the foundation of such a salad. Experiment with combining your favorite vegetables and proteins with any of the grains in this cookbook to eat hot or cold.

KASHA AND RED SPLIT LENTILS

Kasha and lentils each have strong and earthy flavors. When combined with colorful and sweet vegetables, they create a robust and delicious meal. A small portion makes a super snack.

Roasted buckwheat is called **kasha.** *It is not a true grain, but rather a fruit seed that is related to rhubarb. Even though its name suggests otherwise, it does not contain wheat, and is in fact gluten free. Kasha can become mushy and lose its shape and texture when cooked, so it is best to purchase it as a coarse granule for savory grain dishes. The fine or medium granules would work well for a hot breakfast cereal.*

Yield: 4 servings

Instructions

1. Heat oven to 375°F.
2. Remove the stems from the chard and cut the leaves into bite-sized pieces. Rinse in a colander under running water and set aside.
3. Peel and dice the onion and carrot, and sauté with olive oil in a large skillet over medium-high heat for 5 minutes.
4. Add the chard to the skillet and wilt the leaves for 3 minutes. Stir in the kasha and lentils.
5. Add broth, water, paprika, garlic powder and salt. Stir and pour into an 8x8" baking dish.
6. Cover the dish and bake for 30 minutes. When the liquid has been absorbed, the dish is done.

1 bunch or 2 cups chard
2 tablespoons olive oil
1 medium onion
1 medium carrot
½ cup coarse kasha
¼ cup red split lentils
1½ cups vegetable broth
1 cup water
½ teaspoon paprika/smoked paprika
¼ teaspoon garlic powder
½ teaspoon salt

Variations

- Any green vegetable would complement the colors and textures in this dish: chard, spinach, collard greens or broccoli would work. Or, omit all vegetables except for the onions and carrots.
- Sprinkle some crumbled goat cheese or feta on top after taking it out of the oven, or before the last 5 minutes of baking.

THAI TOFU WITH VEGETABLES AND BLACK RICE, p. 42

CHAPTER FOUR: POWERFUL PROTEINS

"You are what you eat eats." –Michael Pollan, *Food Rules*

Protein is an essential component of any balanced diet. It keeps the immune system functioning, and maintains healthy skin, hair, nails and internal organs including the brain and heart. While each person requires different amounts and types of protein to feel strong and energetic, the goal should be to choose high-quality foods that agree with one's body and beliefs.

Chicken, eggs, turkey, beef, fish, beans, edamame (baby soybeans), dairy products, nuts, seeds and tofu are high-quality proteins that are included in this book. Other good sources of protein include seafood and veggie burgers.

Tips for buying high-quality proteins:

- Buy the products of organically-raised animals, including eggs and dairy, to avoid consuming the antibiotics and hormones that are fed to conventionally-raised animals.

- Select fish containing the lowest amounts of mercury including salmon, flounder, sole, sardines and tilapia, and seafood including shrimp and scallops. Avoid fish species that are high in mercury such as King mackerel, swordfish and orange roughy, and limit your intake of canned albacore and yellowfin tuna, grouper and Chilean sea bass.[8]

- Include some nuts, seeds, soybeans and/or legumes in your diet, as they are good sources of protein as well as healthy fats and fiber.

RECIPES

TIME MANAGEMENT AS A TOOL FOR HEALTHY EATING

"The most remarkable thing about my mother is that for thirty years she served the family nothing but leftovers. The original meal has never been found." —Calvin Trillin

One of the main goals of this book is to help you to incorporate more natural foods into your diet, and to teach you strategies to create new supporting habits. Even armed with new knowledge and recipes, it can still be challenging to make the time to shop and cook. It's understandable that your good intentions often become sidelined by the many demands of a busy life. To combat this, you need a time management plan that will help you to implement and support a healthy way of eating and living.

Simply stated, the plan is to make a habit of cooking the individual parts of your meal in quantity so that you will save time throughout the week by repurposing the vegetables, grains, and proteins into meals and snacks rather than cooking every meal from scratch. This kind of preparation is key to managing your time, health and even your food expenditures, so that you will become less dependent on eating out and/or consuming a disproportionate amount of processed food. Cooking in larger quantities sets you up to shorten meal assembly time in subsequent days, and to take control over what you plan to eat.

Notice the Difference

As you try new foods, possibly replacing old regulars, you might discover that you feel better, more energized and less symptomatic of any health issues. For example, if you try the non-dairy or gluten-free ingredients suggested in the recipes and you notice that you are less congested or have fewer headaches, you might decide to continue swapping out the allergen-containing offenders. Or perhaps by adding more leafy greens and other vegetables, and reducing refined and processed carbs, your digestion noticeably improves. Perhaps by eating more root vegetables and fruits, and fewer processed sweets, your sugar cravings decrease. Without being able to pinpoint why, perhaps you have more overall energy and your mood has lifted. Whatever way in which your health is shifting, even if it is subtle, know that your food has the power to heal, and your body is giving you that feedback.

See the following chart for an example of how this strategy works. If you think of vegetables, grains and proteins as your food "wardrobe," you can conceive of myriad "outfits" or combinations. Add spices and flavorings like fashion accessories, and you will never get bored with the look and taste of your food. Plus, it will always fit you!

TIME MANAGEMENT CHART

The chart below shows that cooking in advance and in larger quantities can help to create future meals and snacks. The objective is to ensure that more meals are homemade, nutritious, and can be prepared quickly. If so, you will enable yourself to become less dependent on restaurant and processed food, and you will learn to take control of the quality and variety of your weekly diet.

Bold = A Cookbook Recipe
Italics = Leftover food used to create a new dish

	Breakfast	Lunch	Snack	Dinner
Sunday	**Eggs, Garbanzo Beans & Kale**	**Sweet Broccoli Soup** made with yellow flesh yam	**Chocolate Granola** + fruit	Chicken + **Coconut Millet** + **Mediterranean Medley**
Monday	*Coconut Millet hot cereal* + nuts, raisins	*Garbanzo beans* atop green salad	*Sweet Broccoli Soup*	**Roasted Salmon with Honey Dill Sauce** + brown rice + **French-Cut Green Beans**
Tuesday	**Oatmeal** or plain cereal with *granola*	*Salmon* + *kale* in a wrap	*Yam* + nuts and/or butter	*Chicken* & *Vegetable Stir-Fry* + **Orange Quinoa**
Wednesday	*Orange Quinoa hot cereal* + bananas	*Mediterranean Medley* + brown rice	**Chocolate Granola** + yogurt	**Turkey and Kale Chili** + **Crunchy Seed Cookies**
Thursday	English muffin with avocado	*Turkey & Kale Chili*	*Crunchy Seed Cookies*	Pasta with seafood + **bok choy Salad with Asian Dressing**
Friday	*Sauteed bok choy* + organic chicken sausage	Veggie burger + salad	Almond butter with apples	*Chard with Fried Pasta* + **feta Cheese**
Saturday	Omelet with *chard* + *feta*	**Barley & Edamame with Spinach Pesto**	**Two Bean Hummus** + carrots + tortilla chips	**Kasha & Red Split Lentils** + **Best Green Smoothie**

TIME MANAGEMENT STRATEGIES:

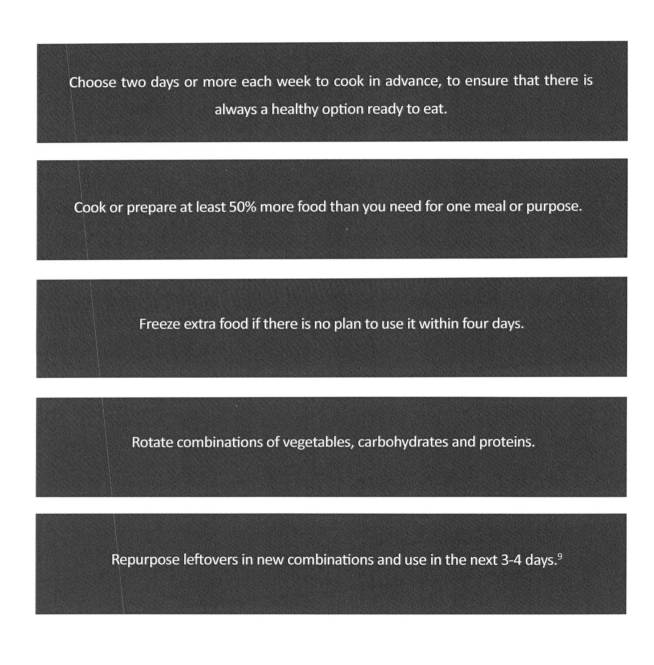

Choose two days or more each week to cook in advance, to ensure that there is always a healthy option ready to eat.

Cook or prepare at least 50% more food than you need for one meal or purpose.

Freeze extra food if there is no plan to use it within four days.

Rotate combinations of vegetables, carbohydrates and proteins.

Repurpose leftovers in new combinations and use in the next 3-4 days.[9]

EGGS, BEANS AND GREENS

This is a good example of a power breakfast. The dense fiber of the beans combined with the protein of the eggs and the uplifting energy of the greens provides long-lasting energy and a satisfying start to the day.

Yield: 2 servings

———————

2-4 eggs
½ cup precooked or 1 cup raw kale, collard greens or chard
½ cup canned beans: black, garbanzo, kidney, etc.
Pan spray, butter, coconut oil or olive oil
Dash of salt and/or garlic powder, onion powder or cumin

———————

Instructions

1. In a small bowl, whisk the eggs. Set aside.
2. Coat a medium frying pan with your choice of fat or oil. Spread cooked greens in the pan in an even layer and warm over medium heat for 2 minutes. **Or,** if using raw greens, remove leaves from the stems and chop into small pieces before adding to the heated pan with ¼ cup water. Cover and sauté the leaves for 3 minutes or until wilted. Drain any remaining water.
3. Add beans and seasonings, cover and continue to cook for 1 minute.
4. Pour eggs into the pan, stirring as the eggs cook. Serve immediately.

Variations

- Add 1-2 tablespoons shredded cheese to the egg mixture. Use cooked vegetables instead of greens, such as broccoli, cauliflower, bell peppers, green beans or asparagus.
- Add the cooked eggs (made with or without beans) to a soft tortilla.

ROASTED SALMON WITH HONEY DILL SAUCE

Dazzle your taste buds with this simple sauce that pairs nicely with any type of fish, particularly salmon. To save time, you may as well roast the vegetables simultaneously. I like to serve this dish with Roasted French-Cut Green Beans (p. 18).

Yield: 4 servings

---

1 lb. salmon fillet, without skin
2 tablespoons extra virgin olive oil
3 tablespoons honey
2 tablespoons balsamic vinegar
½ teaspoon dill, fresh or dried
2 cloves garlic, minced or ½ teaspoon garlic powder
½ teaspoon salt

Instructions

1. Preheat oven to 375°F.
2. Cut the salmon into 4 equal pieces. Place in a baking dish.
3. Combine the olive oil, honey, vinegar, dill, garlic and salt in a small bowl and whisk together.
4. Pour sauce over the fish and place in the oven for approximately 20-25 minutes, or until the flesh separates easily and is completely light pink. Baste the fish with the liquid in the pan once during cooking.

Variations

- Roast tilapia, flounder or sole in place of the salmon, and cook until fish is opaque and flakes with the tines of a fork.
- Replace the dill with your favorite herbs and spices.
- In place of the green beans, broccoli and/or cauliflower can be roasted for 10-15 minutes while the fish is cooking.
- Leftover fish can be cut up and served atop a salad, or added to a stir-fry.

CHICKEN AND VEGETABLE STIR-FRY

This is the best kind of fast food: repurposing leftover chicken in a colorful and nutritious stir-fry in one pan, in just 10 minutes!

Yield: 4 servings

————————

Instructions

1. Cut the broccoli and pepper into bite-sized pieces and set aside. Shred the chicken into bite-sized pieces and set aside.
2. Slice or chop the onion and place in a preheated pan coated with olive oil. Cover and sauté over medium heat for about 2 minutes or until the onions are translucent.
3. Add the broccoli and peppers and cover the pan. Continue to sauté for 2 more minutes.
4. Add the chicken and continue to cook, stirring occasionally for 2 minutes. Serve hot.

1 large crown broccoli
1 orange or red bell pepper
1 cup or more precooked dark or white meat chicken
1 small onion
1 tablespoon olive oil

————————

Variations

- Add 2-3 cups of cooked grains such as rice, quinoa or kasha when heating up the chicken.
- Do the reverse: sauté raw chicken in a skillet coated with oil, and add precooked vegetables and/or grains before the last two minutes of cooking.
- Omit the chicken and enjoy as a vegetable side dish.

THAI TOFU WITH VEGETABLES AND BLACK RICE

Pictured on p. 34

This recipe creates a wholesome meal, but its individual parts could also be eaten separately in different leftover combinations. For example, the rice that is prepared here is more than enough for this recipe and can be repurposed for another meal. The peanut sauce adds a burst of flavor to the whole meal.

Yield: 2 servings

Instructions

1. Rinse rice in a strainer and place in a medium pot with the water and coconut milk. Bring to a boil, then turn the heat down to low and simmer for approximately 40 minutes or until liquid is absorbed. Rice will be done when water no longer runs out from the bottom when the pot is tilted to its side.
2. To make the sauce, whisk together the peanut butter, garlic, orange juice and soy sauce in a small bowl. Add an additional teaspoon of soy sauce if desired. Gradually add more orange juice until the sauce is pourable but still thick. Set aside.
3. Drain tofu and wrap with paper towels, gently squeezing to remove the excess water. Repeat several times until the tofu feels less waterlogged.
4. Cut the tofu lengthwise into thirds and then stack the pieces. Cut the sliced tofu in half on a diagonal, and then in half again in the opposite direction so that you have 4 stacks of 3 triangles each.
5. Heat a large frying pan coated with 2 tablespoons oil over medium-high heat and place the tofu pieces in the pan. Fry for 5 minutes, or until slightly browned on each side.

1 cup black rice
1 cup water
1 cup coconut milk
1 lb. block of firm or extra-firm tofu in water
2 tablespoons + 2 teaspoons olive oil, divided
2 tablespoons soy sauce or gluten-free tamari
6 baby bok choy
1 cup sliced carrots

Sauce:
¼ cup smooth natural peanut butter
1 medium clove garlic
¼ cup orange juice, plus more as needed
2 teaspoons soy sauce or gluten-free tamari, plus more as needed

---

Drizzle 1 tablespoon of soy sauce per side over the tofu while it's cooking. Place cooked tofu in a covered serving dish and set aside.
6. Rinse the bok choy, cut off bottom ends and discard. Cut remaining stalks and leaves into pieces.
7. Add carrots to the pan plus 2 teaspoons of oil and sauté for 3 minutes on medium heat. Add the bok choy, cover the pan and continue to cook for 2 minutes.
8. Fill your plate with ⅓ vegetables, ⅓ tofu and ⅓ rice, and drizzle sauce over the dish.

Variations

• Any leafy greens or vegetables could be used here. Likewise, any grain could replace the rice.

BEEF AND SNOW PEA SAUTÉ

Preparing lunch or dinner can be as simple and quick as sautéing two main ingredients, and then finishing the dish with leftover grains.

Yield: 2 servings

Pan spray
½ lb. minute steak or beef tenderloin
Dash of salt and/or black pepper
2 teaspoons olive oil
6 oz. snow peas
**2 tablespoons *Annie's* balsamic vinegar
     salad dressing**

Instructions

1. Heat a large skillet coated with pan spray on medium heat. With a knife or kitchen scissors, cut beef into 2-inch pieces and place in pan. Add a dash of salt and pepper. Cover the pan and sauté for 2-3 minutes on both sides. Drain the beef and set aside in a bowl.

2. Coat pan with the olive oil and place over medium heat. Sauté the snow peas for 2 minutes. When the snow peas are softened and lightly browned, return the beef to the pan and stir in the salad dressing until the meat and vegetables are coated completely.

Variations

- Any "sturdy" vegetable such as broccoli, cauliflower, carrots or green beans can complement this dish, on its own or in combination.
- To complete the dish, combine 1½ cups precooked millet, brown rice, quinoa or kasha with the beef when returning it to the skillet to heat through.
- Instead of the bottled salad dressing, try a drizzle of soy sauce and a dash of garlic powder or cayenne.

THREE BEAN SALAD

A bean salad can be served as a snack or a meal with the addition of vegetables and grains. Save time by mincing the vegetables in a food processor.

Yield: 4 servings

_____

Instructions

In a small bowl, combine the mustard, lime juice, vinegar, salt, olive oil, radishes, scallions and parsley. Add more of any ingredient to suit your tastes. Pour the dressing over the beans and stir to combine. Serve immediately, or let the ingredients meld in the refrigerator for a few hours before serving.

3 12 oz. cans of beans: white, black, red, pinto or garbanzo

Dressing:
2 tablespoons mustard
Juice of 1 lime
2 tablespoons rice vinegar or balsamic vinegar
1½ teaspoons salt
3 tablespoons extra virgin olive oil
4 radishes, diced or minced
3 scallions, green parts only, minced
2 tablespoons fresh parsley

_____

Variations

- Add ½-1 cup of cooked broccoli, cauliflower or kale cut into small pieces, and/or 2 cups of cooked rice or quinoa, to create a more substantial snack or meal.

CHAPTER FIVE: SATISFYING SOUPS

Soup is the most flexible, diverse and forgiving of recipe categories. Almost anything can be made into or added to a soup: one or a combination of vegetables, fruit, grains, beans, tofu, animal protein and spices, plus water or broth. You can adhere to a recipe or reformulate it with leftover food or whatever ingredients you have on hand. Furthermore, soup fits the criteria of what health-conscious, busy people are seeking perfectly: food with nutritious ingredients that is easy and quick to prepare, and that is adjustable to individual tastes.

RECIPES

A SHORTCUT TO SMARTER EATING: CHEW MORE

*For those who like instant gratification and want a healthy eating tip, here's a good one: chew more. Most of us rush through the whole eating process because we are in a hurry, or simply do so out of habit. We also eat while we're distracted—working, reading, talking and watching television—and swallow food practically whole. However, if you were to thoroughly **chew** your food, you could improve your health on a daily basis. It's not just what you eat, but **how** you eat that matters.*

Digestion Begins with the First Bite

Digestion actually begins in the mouth, where contact with your teeth and digestive enzymes in your saliva begin to break down the food. Aim for at least 20-30 chews for every bite, or chew until the food is liquid.[10] This will sufficiently prepare the food for further digestion and assimilation into the body. Such a strategy requires a longer mealtime, and a change in mindset that reminds you to slow down.

Slow Down and Reap the Benefits

Thoroughly chewing your food will reward you in many ways and motivate you to maintain the habit. In the beginning, you have to set your intention to practice chewing, but you will soon notice its many benefits: [11, 12]

- Thoroughly chewing reduces the work that the stomach has to do, and can significantly **lessen fatigue** after a meal.

- Predigesting makes the food sweeter because chewing breaks down the molecules of starch in the food, which enhances the taste and can **decrease cravings** for desserts.

- More chewing produces **more endorphins,** the chemicals released in the brain that are responsible for creating good feelings. You may experience a slight high after eating.

- Chewing promotes **weight loss,** because it gives your stomach more time to communicate to your brain when you are full. When you eat more slowly, you are more likely to pay attention to how much you are eating and how your stomach is feeling. Thus, you end up eating less.

- The concentration required to slow down a meal can **reduce stress, increase relaxation and restore mental energy.**

Practice thoroughly chewing your food at one meal every day, or for part of two meals, and do more with time. If you are able to consistently increase your chewing, you may experience a notable difference in your health!

BUTTERNUT SQUASH SOUP

It is easy to produce a delicious and impressive soup from the sweet, dense butternut squash. Its beautiful orange color and spicy aroma make it a crowd-pleaser for any occasion.

Yield: 4 servings

1 onion, chopped
1 tablespoon olive oil
1 large butternut squash, peeled and cubed (or 20 oz. precut butternut squash)
1 cup chopped carrots
1½ teaspoons grated fresh ginger
½ teaspoon cinnamon
1 teaspoon salt, plus more to taste
1½-2 cups water or vegetable broth
Pumpkin seeds for garnish

Instructions

1. Sauté the onions in the olive oil in a soup pot until they become translucent.
2. Add squash, carrots, ginger, cinnamon, salt and about 1½ cups water (less is better to start–you can always add more liquid at the end if the soup is too thick). Cover and bring to a boil on high heat, then reduce to low and simmer for 15 minutes.
3. Stir occasionally. Soup will be done when the tip of a knife easily pierces the biggest pieces of squash.
4. Cool completely (or partially) to avoid burning yourself when blending. Working in batches if necessary, ladle the mixture into a blender or food processor and blend until smooth. Set blended soup aside and repeat with the remaining soup. An immersion blender could also be used directly in the soup pot.
5. Add more water to reach the desired consistency and salt to taste if necessary. Return

to the soup pot and reheat for a few minutes.
6. To toast the pumpkin seeds, place on a small baking sheet in a 350°F oven for 5 minutes. Sprinkle a tablespoon of seeds on top of each bowl of soup and serve.

Variations

- Replace carrots with 1 cup or more of parsnips, acorn squash or yams, plus an additional ½ cup of water.
- Various spices can complement this recipe. Add ¼ teaspoon garlic powder, nutmeg, allspice or cardamom in addition to the cinnamon.

BLACK BEAN AND VEGETABLE SOUP

This soup makes a great winter side dish or main course, and provides another way to incorporate the fiber- and protein-rich black bean into your diet.

Yield: 4-6 servings

_____

2 tablespoons olive oil
1 cup chopped onions
4 cloves garlic, minced or pressed
2 cups diced carrots
2 teaspoons ground cumin
1 teaspoon salt, plus more to taste
1 cup diced celery
1 cup chopped broccoli
2 15 oz. cans black beans
2 cups diced fresh tomatoes, or 14 oz. can diced tomatoes
½ cup fresh or frozen corn
1 cup water or vegetable broth

_____

Instructions

1. Coat a soup pot with oil and place over medium heat. Sauté the onions and garlic for about 10 minutes or until the onions are translucent, stirring frequently.
2. Add the carrots, cumin and salt. Cook on medium heat for 5 minutes, stirring often.
3. Add the celery and broccoli. Lower the heat, cover and cook for about 10 minutes.
4. Add the beans, tomatoes, corn and water. Simmer covered for 25 minutes, stirring occasionally. If using fresh tomatoes, simmer the soup for an additional 5 minutes.
5. Taste the soup and add salt or other spices if needed.

_____

Variations

- Try green bell peppers instead of broccoli, and/ or yams instead of carrots.

SWEET BROCCOLI SOUP

Parsnips and sweet potatoes add texture and sweetness to this soup, and allow the broccoli to show off its beautiful green and healthy assets.

Yield: 4 servings

————————

Instructions

1. Roughly chop the onion and add it to a heavy soup pot with a drizzle of olive oil. Sauté over medium heat for 3-4 minutes.
2. Peel the parsnips and yam and cut into 2-inch pieces. Cut broccoli into similar-sized chunks. Place the vegetables in the pot and add water or broth to ⅔ the height of the vegetables. Add salt and a 2-inch piece of raw peeled ginger, and cover.
3. Bring to a boil, then turn down to low and simmer for 12-15 minutes or until a knife pierces the vegetables easily.
4. Cool completely (or partially) to avoid burning yourself when blending. Working in batches if necessary, ladle the mixture into a blender or food processor and blend until smooth. Set blended soup aside and repeat with the remaining soup. An immersion blender could

1 small onion
Extra virgin olive oil
2 medium to large parsnips
1 large yellow flesh yam
1 large crown broccoli
2 cups water or vegetable/chicken broth
1 teaspoon salt
2-inch piece raw ginger (optional)
1 tablespoon butter or coconut spread (optional)

————————

also be used directly in the soup pot.
5. Stir blended soup to combine and add salt to taste. Add water or broth to reach the desired consistency. Add butter or coconut spread to taste. Reheat on the stove on low heat for 1-2 minutes and serve hot.

————————

Variations

- A Yukon gold potato can fill in for the yellow flesh yam, but the soup will still be sweet.

————————

Yellow flesh yams can often be found at small produce or specialty markets.

WHITE BEAN AND TOMATO SOUP

This combination of potatoes, beans and tomatoes makes a comforting and hearty snack or a light meal.

Yield: 4-6 servings

———————

Instructions

1. Roughly chop the onion and add it to a heavy soup pot with a drizzle of olive oil. Sauté on medium-low heat for 2-3 minutes.
2. Add the diced carrot and potato to the pot and continue sautéing for 3 minutes, stirring a few times.
3. Add the parsley, salt, pepper, beans, tomatoes and water and cover the pot. Bring to a boil on medium-high heat, then lower heat to simmer uncovered for 25-30 minutes, stirring occasionally.
4. Cool completely (or partially) to avoid burning yourself when blending. Working in batches if necessary, ladle ¾ of the soup into a blender or food processor and blend until

1 small onion
1-2 tablespoons extra virgin olive oil
2 small carrots, diced
1 Yukon gold potato, diced
1 tablespoon chopped parsley
½ teaspoon salt
¼ teaspoon black pepper
2 15 oz. cans navy beans
1 cup or 8 oz. can diced tomatoes
3 cups water or vegetable/chicken broth

———————

smooth. Add the blended soup back to the remaining unblended soup and stir well. Add more liquid if soup is too thick.
5. Add more salt or pepper to taste.

———————

Variations

- Cannellini beans, butter beans, or any kind of white canned bean could be used in this recipe.
- Red, new or fingerling potatoes can be substituted for the Yukon gold.

TURKEY AND KALE CHILI

I like chili because it is dense and textured. Like many soups, chili provides an opportunity to add precooked or raw vegetables that you have on hand to complete the soup. You can add your favorite hot spices as well. Try a new variation of the original recipe every time you make it.

Yield: 4-6 servings

Instructions

1. Preheat a large skillet coated with 1 tablespoon olive oil on medium heat. Add the ground turkey and salt to the pan and cook, stirring frequently. Add tomatoes and tomato paste and heat through on low heat.
2. Meanwhile, heat 1 tablespoon oil in a large soup pot on medium-low heat. Sauté the onions and garlic for 3 minutes.
3. Add the carrots, chili powder and cumin to the soup pot, and sauté for 2 minutes.
4. Add the turkey and tomato mixture to the soup pot.
5. Add beans and water and cook on medium heat until boiling. Reduce heat to low and continue to simmer for 15-20 minutes.
6. Add kale and simmer for 5 minutes. Serve immediately.

2 tablespoons olive oil, divided
½-¾ lb. ground turkey
1 teaspoon salt
1 14½ oz. can roasted diced tomatoes
¼ cup tomato paste
1 medium onion, chopped
3 cloves garlic, minced
1 cup carrots, sliced
1 tablespoon chili powder
1 teaspoon ground cumin
1 15 oz. can kidney or cannellini beans
3 cups water
2 cups shredded kale leaves, stems removed

Variations

- Celery, broccoli and corn could replace, or be added to the pot at the same time as, the carrots.
- Collard greens could replace the kale. Any precooked vegetables could be added to the pot at the same time as the leafy greens.
- Ground beef could replace the turkey, or 1 additional cup of beans could replace the meat.

CHAPTER SIX: HEALTHY SNACKS AND DIPS

"The basic principles of good diets are so simple that I can summarize them in just ten words: eat less, move more, eat lots of fruits and vegetables. For additional clarification, a five-word modifier helps: go easy on junk foods."
–Marion Nestle, *What to Eat*

Healthy snack food: is that an oxymoron? It doesn't have to be. A good snack is not a dessert, which is generally sweet and calorie dense, and nutrient devoid. A snack should be a bridge between meals that is always nutrient dense. Over the past 25 years in the US, snacks have spread to all parts of our day, removing the desire for proper, well-balanced meals. We have also been given permission by some well-meaning medical professionals to eat small meals throughout the day, to better balance our blood sugar. Food manufacturers have filled in that "need" with myriad empty-calorie, fatty, salty and sweet products. We can do better than this,

and healthy snacking can be just as satisfying and habit forming.

A snack should contain components of a nutritious meal: vegetables or fruits, healthy fats, whole grains or protein. It should have little, if any, added sugar. A healthy snack can even be a leftover or small portion of your lunch or dinner. Some of the recipes found in the following pages can stand alone, whereas others are best paired with another wholesome food that will fuel you with high-quality energy. See Eating On-the-Go or at Work (p. 54) for a list of healthy snack options.

RECIPES

EATING ON-THE-GO OR AT WORK

Healthy snacks and small meals

In the Desk Drawer or Handbag	In the Office Refrigerator	In the Office Microwave
Apple, banana, clementine, pear, etc.	Carrots or sliced vegetables with hummus or guacamole	Baked sweet potato/squash
Whole grain crackers or tortilla chips with salsa or hummus	Peanut or almond butter on whole grain crackers or apple slices	Microwave popcorn (choose a brand with no trans fats)
Trail mix (nuts, seeds, dried fruit)	Precooked veggie burger on whole grain bread	Homemade or canned soup (watch the sodium)
Pomegranate seeds	Dinner leftovers of roasted salmon and French-cut green beans	Dinner leftovers of cooked kale, fish and quinoa
Granola or KIND bars with <6 grams sugar	Plain unsweetened yogurt/cottage cheese mixed with fresh berries, apples, bananas or nuts	Plain oatmeal with a handful of nuts or raisins
Rice cakes and organic peanut butter	Brown rice and bean salad	Frozen or reheated vegetables to supplement lunch
Travel-size Wholly Guacamole with tortilla chips or rice cakes	Sliced turkey and baby spinach on whole grain bread or tuna, egg or chicken salad	Frozen low-fat meal
Crunchy Seed Cookies	Cottage cheese with cut fruit	Dinner leftovers of chicken and vegetable stir-fry with rice

Keep snacking portions small.

CHUNKY GUACAMOLE

The avocado has become a staple in our diets, mainly in the form of guacamole. My favorite version is flavorful and chunky, making it a hearty dip or spread to serve with vegetables or tortilla chips.

Yield: 4 servings

————————

Instructions

1. Place onion and garlic in a food processor to finely dice. Add avocado and blend ingredients together, scraping down sides of the food processor once or twice.
2. Add lime juice and tomato and process again. Add salt to taste and process until the desired consistency is reached.
3. Serve chilled with sliced raw vegetables or tortilla chips.

¼ small red onion
1 clove garlic, or ¼ teaspoon garlic powder
1 large peeled and pitted Haas avocado
       (black-skinned)
1 tablespoon lime or lemon juice
⅓ cup diced tomato
Salt

————————

Variations

- Other ingredients to flavor the guacamole could include cilantro, chives, scallions or cayenne.
- Leftovers can be used as a topping on toast, or can be mixed into warm rice or pasta.

————————

If preparing in advance, refrigerate with plastic wrap touching the dip to protect from air exposure and prevent browning.

CHOCOLATE GRANOLA

This is a double recipe since I expect that you'll be using a lot of this granola. Add it to yogurt, cereal, trail mix, salad, fruit, or eat it on its own! Most commercial granolas are overly sweet and may not be customized with your favorite ingredients.

Yield: 4 servings

Instructions

1. Preheat oven to 325°F. Grease two baking sheets with pan spray.
2. Place the nuts, oats, cereal, chocolate chips, seeds, cinnamon and salt in a large bowl and mix together.
3. In a small saucepan on low heat, warm the oil, vanilla and brown rice syrup. Stir to combine with a whisk for 1-2 minutes, or until liquids are blended.
4. Slowly pour the warm liquid over the mixture, folding it in until all of the ingredients are evenly coated.
5. Spread the granola evenly between the prepared baking sheets and bake for 20 minutes.
6. Remove from oven momentarily to flip mixture over. Swap the position of the baking sheets to evenly distribute the heat when returning to the oven. Bake for another 10 minutes or until golden brown.

1 cup coarsely chopped almonds, walnuts, and/or pecans
4 cups rolled oats
3 cups *Rice Chex,* crispy rice cereal or a combination of both
¼ cup mini dark chocolate chips
½ cup sunflower or pumpkin seeds
2 teaspoons cinnamon
1 teaspoon salt
⅓ cup canola oil
1½ teaspoons pure vanilla extract
1 cup *Lundberg's* brown rice syrup

---

7. Allow granola to cool completely on the baking sheets. Break up the granola into small chunks or pieces with your hands. Store in a container with a tight-fitting lid at room temperature, or refrigerate in plastic ware.

Variations

- If you cannot find brown rice syrup at the grocery store or health food store, use one or a combination of ¾ cup total honey, pure maple syrup or agave syrup.
- For a gluten-free version, use *Trader Joe's* or *Bob's Red Mill* gluten-free oats and the gluten-free version of *Kellogg's Rice Krispies* in the yellow box with a gluten-free banner on the label; for dairy-free granola, use *Enjoy Life* or *Chocolate Dream* chocolate chips.

NUTTY POTATOES

Sweet potatoes or yams are not just for side dishes, but can stand alone as a satisfying snack, especially if nuts are sprinkled on top to add crunch and extra protein. To add a smooth nutty flavor, almond butter sauce can be drizzled on top.

What grocery stores commonly call a yam, with orange skin and flesh, is technically a sweet potato. What you might refer to as a sweet potato, with yellow or white flesh and a drier texture, is botanically a yam. No matter how you refer to them, for this recipe I consider these two varieties of tuber to be interchangeable in terms of taste and desirability.

Yield: 6 servings

---

3 orange sweet potatoes or yellow flesh yams
Butter or dairy-free alternative
6 tablespoons chopped walnuts, almonds or pecans
Dash of cinnamon
Salt to taste

Sauce:
⅓ cup almond butter
1 tablespoon fresh grated ginger
1 tablespoon soy sauce or gluten-free tamari
2 tablespoons agave syrup, maple syrup or honey
1 tablespoon rice vinegar, white wine, lime juice, or your favorite acidic liquid ingredient

---

Instructions

1. Preheat oven to 425°F.
2. Wash the sweet potatoes and pat dry. With the tip of a knife, prick each potato all over about 6 times.
3. Place potatoes in the oven on a baking sheet lined with aluminum foil. Roast for 45-55 minutes, or until a knife pierces the potatoes easily.
4. If eating immediately without the optional sauce, cut potatoes in half lengthwise. Any potatoes that you will not be using immediately should remain whole. Add a dab of butter to each half and sprinkle a tablespoon of nuts on top.
5. If you are making the sauce, whisk together the almond butter, ginger, soy sauce, sweetener and vinegar while the potatoes are baking. Taste and adjust the quantity of ingredients accordingly. Drizzle 2 tablespoons of sauce on each cooked potato.

6. If you are not going to serve all of the potatoes at once, allow the leftover potatoes to cool and wrap them individually in aluminum foil. Leftover sauce may require the addition of 1-2 tablespoons of water to thin it out before using again.
7. When reheating potatoes, place in a 350°F oven for 10 minutes or until warmed through, and top with nuts or leftover sauce.

Variations

- Cut the cooked sweet potatoes, with skins intact, into small chunks to add to a vegetable stir-fry or a premade soup.

TWO BEAN HUMMUS

Hummus is so easy to make at home and to customize to suit your tastes! This version uses the traditional garbanzo beans as well as white beans and spices to tantalize the taste buds.

Yield: 8-10 servings

¾ cup canned cannellini beans
1 cup canned garbanzo beans
1 tablespoon tahini
Juice of ½ lemon
1-2 medium cloves garlic
Dash of paprika/smoked paprika
½ teaspoon ground cumin
½ teaspoon salt

Instructions

1. Drain the beans, reserving the liquid from the garbanzo beans.

2. In a food processor, blend all ingredients except the reserved liquid. Add the reserved liquid a tablespoon at a time until the hummus reaches the desired consistency, using approximately 3-4 tablespoons of the reserved liquid in total. Adjust seasonings to taste.

Variations

- The tahini can be substituted with olive oil.
- Other spices to try: ¼-½ teaspoon cayenne, red pepper flakes or curry powder.

BEST GREEN SMOOTHIE

The surprise ingredients in this refreshing and tasty smoothie are the spinach, which adds a velvety texture and emerald color without any noticeable bitterness, and the almond butter, which adds depth of flavor and a dose of healthy fat and protein. Finally, the yellow fruit make this drink bright and sweet. It's the best green smoothie ever!

Yield: 2 servings

1 ripe frozen banana, peeled and cut into 2-inch chunks (peel, slice and freeze banana ahead of time)
6 oz. cold milk or rice/almond milk, more as needed
Big handful of baby spinach, or regular spinach with stems removed
1 cup frozen mango and/or pineapple
1-2 tablespoons almond butter

Instructions

1. Combine banana and milk in a blender and whirl at top speed for approximately 30 seconds.
2. Add spinach and blend for 30 seconds. Add the fruit and blend for 30 seconds. Add almond butter and blend until smooth. If consistency is too thick to pour, add ½ cup of water or milk. Serve immediately.

Variations

- Try kale with the stems removed instead of spinach.
- Try a combination of fresh and frozen fruit, including peaches, kiwi, nectarines, apples, and pears, to maintain the green color.

CRUNCHY SEED COOKIES

Nuts and seeds provide richness and a crunchy texture to this surprisingly filling snack, in addition to healthy fats, protein and minerals. These cookies could be eaten alone or broken into pieces and added to a creamy snack of yogurt or cottage cheese.

Yield: 12 1-inch cookies

----

1 cup sunflower seeds, unsalted
½ cup pumpkin seeds, unsalted
1 tablespoon chia seeds (optional)
⅛ teaspoon salt
1½ tablespoons canola oil
3 tablespoons honey
1 tablespoon raisins

Instructions

1. Preheat oven to 325°F.
2. Combine sunflower, pumpkin and chia seeds and salt, and blend together in a food processor until half the mixture has reached the consistency of flour and the other half still retains its texture.
3. Measure the oil and pour into the mixture. Measure the honey in the same cup, as the residual oil will allow it to slide out easily. Add raisins and pulse to combine.
4. Form 12 1-inch balls with a mini scoop or by rolling in your palm. Place on a greased baking sheet at least an inch apart, then flatten slightly.
5. Bake for 15 minutes or until golden. Cool for 10 minutes before removing from baking sheet.

Variations

- Any combination of nuts and seeds will work as long as a floury texture is achieved.
- Other sweeteners to try are brown rice syrup or agave syrup.
- Try dried blueberries or cranberries in place of the raisins.

CHAPTER SEVEN: WHOLESOME DESSERTS

"Take care of your body. It's the only place you have to live."
–Jim Rohn, author and motivational speaker

Eating dessert is part of our culture, helping us to celebrate life in the big and small moments. However, we should consider limiting sweet foods to special occasions, comprising a small percentage of our overall consumption. The United States Department of Agriculture (USDA) reported in 2010 that the average American consumes anywhere between 150 to 170 pounds of refined sugars in one year![13,14] Eating desserts and consuming too much sugar in our drinks and snacks, as well as added sugar in thousands of everyday food products, is our collective downfall. Excessive sugar contributes to many unwanted health issues such as weight gain, diabetes, hyperactivity, brain fog, weakened immune systems, fatigue and more.

If you practice taking the very best care of yourself, then a balanced eating plan may occasionally include treating yourself to desserts made with wholesome ingredients. It's possible to love yourself and have your dessert in the same bite.

RECIPES

BANANA CHOCOLATE CHIP MUFFINS, p. 67

SIX REMEDIES FOR COMMON EATING MISTAKES

With all of the nutrition advice available on the Internet and in the media, why do savvy food consumers who eat healthy foods like salmon, broccoli, whole grain pasta and salads struggle with ongoing health issues? Concerns with weight, fatigue, food cravings, digestive distress and pain are quite common. Where is this disconnect created between the knowledge and the action?

Here are the most common mistakes that I observe in my practice, and some suggestions for remedying them:

1. Filling up a large dinner plate with a variety of foods, at home or at a restaurant, often results in overeating. Even if it looks balanced, an oversized plate with too much of anything on it (except for vegetables) adds up to too many calories.

Try this: Fill half of your plate with vegetables, add a fist-sized portion of meat or protein and a "golf ball" or two of whole grains.

2. Vegetarians, and those who choose to cut back on meat to avoid saturated fat, often replace protein with mostly starches. This can lead to an imbalanced diet and an accumulation of body fat.

Try this: Instead of filling up on starch, replace with other types of protein, such as tofu or tempeh, beans, veggie burgers, nuts and seeds, yogurt, eggs or fish. Limit breads and starches to one third of your total diet.

3. In an effort to lose weight, many people skip breakfast or lunch and end up eating "backwards." That is, they eat most of their food at the end of the day when metabolism often slows down, and eat the least in the mornings when metabolism is the fastest.

Try this: "Eat breakfast like a king, lunch like a prince and dinner like a pauper." —Adelle Davis

4. Food manufacturers have contributed to redefining a snack as a dessert or empty-calorie food. Choosing 100-calorie cookie packages, for example, is a lost opportunity to consume food that's rich in nutrients, fiber, and energy-rich protein.

Try this: Whole, unprocessed foods like raw vegetables and fruits, and small amounts of meat, beans or whole grains, should be used to bridge your meals.

5. Heeding popular advice to eat small meals throughout the day, people are "grazing" (i.e. filling up on salty and sweet snacks) and are consequently consuming fewer nutrients and more calories.

Try this: Eat three substantial meals a day that include mostly vegetables and proteins with some carbohydrates and fruits, and very small snacks.

6. Eating so-called nutritious food—such as whole wheat products, sweetened yogurt and "sugar-free" items—can make people feel sick or weak because of food sensitivities to gluten, dairy or artificial sweeteners.

Try this: Eliminate one kind of food at a time to see if you feel better, or seek guidance from a trained professional to help you identify the source and find where it is hidden in other foods.

Small shifts in your eating habits can add up to a big difference in your health and wellbeing.

NO-BAKE FRUIT PIE

This versatile fruit pie requires no baking and is easy and quick to assemble. The dates hold the nuts together to form the crust. Choose fruit that is in season and enjoy the sweet taste of this refreshing dessert!

Yield: 6-8 servings

————————

5 cups sliced seasonal fruit, or 1½ lbs.
    fresh strawberries, quartered + 1
    cup blueberries
2 tablespoons orange juice or lemon juice
1 teaspoon pure vanilla extract
1 tablespoon agave syrup
1 tablespoon pure maple syrup
Pinch of salt

Crust:
2 cups raw almonds
½ teaspoon cinnamon
1½ cups pitted dates
1 tablespoon water

Instructions

1. Combine fruit, orange juice, vanilla, sweeteners and salt in a bowl and toss to combine. Set aside while you make the crust.
2. Coat with pan spray or lightly oil a 9-inch pie plate.
3. Place almonds and cinnamon in a food processor and pulse until they resemble breadcrumbs. Set aside in a bowl.
4. Place dates and water in the food processor and pulse until well chopped and a little clumpy.
5. Add the almonds back to the food processor and pulse until combined.
6. Press the sticky mixture evenly onto the bottom and sides of the pie plate to form the crust.
7. Pour the fruit into the crust. Refrigerate for two hours before slicing into wedges and serving.

————————

Variations

- In the winter, make this pie with 3-4 peeled pears and/or apples, cut into bite-sized chunks.
- Try other combinations of liquid sweeteners such as brown rice syrup or honey.

EASY APPLE CRISP

I love this recipe because it is not overly sweet and has a texture that's both soft and crunchy. Choose any good baking apples such as Rome, Granny Smith, Cortland, McIntosh or a combination of varieties.

Yield: 6 servings

————

**4 medium to large fresh apples, cored and
   sliced
2 tablespoons orange or lemon juice
1 teaspoon pure vanilla extract
½ teaspoon cinnamon
⅛ teaspoon nutmeg
Pinch of salt**

Topping:
**1 cup rolled oats
½ cup walnuts, pecans or almonds
¼ cup *Lundberg's* brown rice syrup
Pinch of salt**

————

Instructions

1. Preheat oven to 350°F.
2. In a large bowl, combine the apples, vanilla, cinnamon, nutmeg and salt. Place in an 8-inch square baking dish.
3. In a food processor, pulse oats until coarsely ground. Transfer to a clean bowl.
4. Pulse nuts in the food processor until they are coarsely ground, and add to the oats.
5. Lubricate the inside of a measuring cup with pan spray or canola oil before measuring the brown rice syrup, so that it will slide out easily into the bowl. Add to the mixture along with a pinch of salt.
6. Combine all of the topping ingredients in the bowl, using vinyl-gloved hands or a wooden spoon to form a sticky dough.
7. Drop the dough by the tablespoonful on top of the fruit, and spread out as evenly as possible.
8. Bake for 30-40 minutes or until the topping is golden brown and fruit is fork tender.
9. Remove from the oven and cool for at least five minutes before serving.

————

Variations

- For a gluten-free version, use oats that are certified gluten free.

PUMPKIN BROWNIES

Sweet to eat just as they are, these brownies make a wholesome dessert any time of year.

Yield: 16 2-inch square bars

_____

Instructions

1. Preheat oven to 350°F. Grease an 8-inch square baking pan with baking spray, or grease with butter and dust with flour.
2. In a large bowl, sift together the flour, baking powder and pumpkin pie spice and set aside.
3. In a standing mixer, cream together the butter and sugar until well blended. Beat in the egg. Add the vanilla and the pumpkin puree and continue to beat until thoroughly mixed.
4. Add the sifted dry ingredients to the pumpkin mixture to form a batter.
5. Fold in the chopped walnuts by hand.
6. Pour the thick batter into the prepared pan and spread it around as evenly as possible.
7. Bake for 30-40 minutes or until a knife or toothpick inserted in the center comes out dry.
8. Cool for about 5 minutes in the pan. Go around the edge of the pan with a knife to separate the

Baking spray (optional)
1 cup whole wheat pastry flour
      or unbleached all-purpose flour
1 teaspoon baking powder
1½ teaspoons pumpkin pie spice
½ cup softened butter or *Earth Balance* coconut spread
½ cup packed light brown sugar
1 egg
1 teaspoon pure vanilla extract
¾ cup canned 100% pure pumpkin
½ cup chopped walnuts (optional)

_____

brownies from the sides. Flip over to remove brownies from the pan and finish cooling on a covered surface or wire rack. After 30 minutes, slice the brownies to create 16 squares.

_____

Variations

- For a gluten-free version, use any gluten-free flour + 1 teaspoon xanthan gum (if it's not already included in the flour mix).
- Add 1 teaspoon of raw grated ginger to the wet mixture.
- Finish brownies with a dusting of confectioners sugar.
- Fold in ½ cup mini dark chocolate chips in place of/in addition to the nuts before baking.

CRISPY RICE TREATS

This is a naturally-sweetened treat that adults will enjoy as much as the kids. Get creative and add different seeds, nuts or dried fruit each time you make these!

Yield: 16-20 2½-inch bars

---

4 cups crispy rice cereal
¼ cup semi-sweet or dark chocolate chips
¾ cup natural peanut butter or almond butter
¾ cup *Lundberg's* brown rice syrup

Instructions

1. In a large bowl, combine cereal with the chocolate chips and any optional ingredients (see variations).
2. Measure nut butter and rice syrup in a measuring cup coated with oil or pan spray so that they will pour out easily from the cup into a small saucepan. Heat them over low heat, stirring occasionally for 2 minutes or until smooth and combined.
3. Pour rice syrup mixture over the cereal mixture and stir to combine thoroughly.
4. Press mixture into an 8x8" or 9x13" glass baking dish or plastic storage container with low sides.
5. Cool for 30 minutes in the refrigerator. Cut into squares. Can be stored in the refrigerator or freezer.

Variations

- Add ¼ cup peanuts, raisins, sunflower seeds or unsweetened shredded coconut to the dry mixture.
- To make a gluten-free version, use *Kellogg's Rice Krispies* in the yellow box with a gluten-free banner on the label.
- To make crispy rice treats that are dairy- and/or soy-free, use *Enjoy Life* or *Chocolate Dream* chocolate chips.

BANANA CHOCOLATE CHIP MUFFINS

Pictured on p. 61

Bananas provide a lot of value to dessert dishes. They add sweetness, fiber and a flavor that most people enjoy. The earthy spices add a depth of flavor and the outcome is a mildly sweet and very satisfying treat. The chocolate chips are included for people who prefer more sweetness, more chocolate, or both.

Yield: 18 muffins or 3 dozen mini muffins

————————

Instructions

1. Preheat oven 350°F. Line muffin tins with paper cups or grease with oil or pan spray.
2. In a large bowl, sift the flour, salt, baking powder, baking soda, allspice, cardamom and cinnamon. Set aside.
3. Measure the canola oil and pour into a standing mixer or large bowl. Then measure the honey in the same cup so that it will slide out easily into the bowl. Add the mashed bananas and mix well.
4. Pour the dry ingredients into the wet ingredients and combine by hand or with the electric mixer. Fold in half of the walnuts and the chocolate chips.
5. Pour into muffin tins. Sprinkle with the reserved walnuts.
6. Bake for 20 minutes or about half that time for mini muffins. Test for doneness by pressing with a finger to see if the center of a muffin bounces back, or determine doneness by inserting a toothpick in the center of a muffin to see if it comes out dry.

2 cups whole wheat pastry flour or unbleached all-purpose flour
½ teaspoon salt
1 teaspoon baking powder
1 teaspoon baking soda
¾ teaspoon allspice
¼ teaspoon cardamom
½ teaspoon cinnamon
⅓ cup canola oil
⅓ cup honey
2¼ cups mashed bananas (from about 5 large ripe bananas)
½ cup finely chopped walnuts, divided
½ cup mini dark chocolate chips

————————

Variations

- For a gluten-free version, use gluten-free flour plus ½ teaspoon xanthan gum (if it's not already included in the flour mix).
- Instead of honey, use ½ cup *Lundberg's* brown rice syrup.
- Omit the chocolate chips and/or the nuts.

CHOCOLATE TRAIL MIX BARK

An easy and creative way to embellish good quality chocolate when you want to impress your guests is to make your own chocolate bark. Enrich each bite with a sweet, crunchy and chewy sensation for a healthy, luscious dessert.

Yield: 10 2-inch pieces

¼ cup chopped walnuts and/or almonds
¼ cup dried blueberries, raisins and/or
    cranberries
2 tablespoons sunflower, pumpkin and/
    or chia seeds
¼ cup crispy rice cereal
3.5 oz. 70-80% dark chocolate bar

Instructions

1. Line a 9x13" baking sheet with parchment paper, waxed paper or aluminum foil.
2. Combine the nuts, dried fruit, seeds and cereal in a small bowl and set aside.
3. Heat the chocolate in a double boiler or an ovenproof bowl set over a pan of simmering water. **Or** microwave at 50% power for 1 minute, then in 30-second intervals until melted, stirring between each. Stir just until the chocolate is melted and smooth, making sure no water gets into the chocolate.
4. Add the dry ingredients to the warm chocolate, stir to combine and immediately pour the mixture onto the prepared baking sheet. Spread the mixture evenly with a spatula.

5. Refrigerate for about 30 minutes until firm. Break the chocolate up into about 10 pieces and store in an airtight container at room temperature or in the refrigerator.

Variations

- Other mix-ins could include 1 tablespoon of shredded coconut or your choice of other nuts, dried fruit and seeds not used in this recipe. Remember to chop larger nuts and dried fruit into very small pieces before stirring into the chocolate.

CHIA SEED PUDDING

The tiny black chia seeds have become a popular super food because of their high fiber, protein and mineral content. Most notably, their ability to absorb 10-12 times their weight in liquid and to become gel-like will help to make you feel full and satisfied. Because chia seeds have a very mild taste, they are easy to incorporate into your diet. Sprinkle them on any food, or mix them into yogurt, smoothies, drinks and hot cereals. I love to eat them by creating puddings that can be mixed together in minutes.

Yield: 4 ½-cup servings

1 cup milk or dairy-free alternative
1 medium ripe banana
⅓ cup fresh or frozen pineapple pieces
2 tablespoons agave syrup or honey
¼ cup chia seeds
Dark chocolate for garnish

Instructions

1. Place the milk, banana, pineapple and sweetener in a blender and process until smooth and well combined.
2. Add chia seeds to the blender and run for 5 seconds.
3. Pour mixture into a lidded container and place in the refrigerator for 2-3 hours to thicken.
4. Garnish the top of each serving with chocolate shavings created by using a vegetable peeler or knife to shave the edge of a chocolate bar.
5. Serve as is, or create a parfait by layering the pudding into serving bowls with sliced fruit in between the layers.

Variations

- Replace the pineapple with fresh or frozen mango, peaches, blueberries, strawberries or papaya.
- Try coconut, soy, almond or rice milk as alternatives to cow's milk.
- For chocolate lovers, add 1 teaspoon unsweetened cocoa powder to the mix.
- Other flavors to add to the mixture: 1 teaspoon grated fresh ginger, 1 teaspoon pure vanilla extract, or 1 tablespoon unsweetened shredded coconut.

FINAL THOUGHTS

The Journey Continues

"Change your thoughts and you change your world."
–Norman Vincent Peale

With this book, you will take some of the first steps in a long and gradual journey toward improving your diet, health and happiness. Whether you incorporate the approach set forth in these pages methodically or in spurts, any small shift helps to move you forward on the path. There is no timetable for change; you set your own pace based on your situation and level of motivation.

What I find inspiring about the power of food is the opportunity to witness the transformations of my clients. The starting point is specific and measured. For example, clients may aim to increase their energy and lose weight, to manage a health condition, or to transition to a gluten-free or otherwise allergen-free diet. A new mindset is acquired that supports an improved eating plan and time management strategies. The individual becomes better, stronger, more energized and more positive.

Then something else happens, both unplanned and uncharted. Feeling in control of their lives, empowered by their success in the kitchen and with self-improvement, my clients start to see a world of opportunity open up before them. They envision change in other areas of their lives that would have seemed unfathomable or too overwhelming to take on in the past. With this new optimism, another set of goals suddenly seems possible and attainable. The experience of taking control of their food and self-care becomes the fuel for ending or starting a relationship, moving to a different home or job, or returning to a rewarding pastime. In short, one positive change begets another, and thus life may become more fulfilling. This book leads readers toward the first steps involved in this process. *Imagine what it could be for you.*

The pursuit of eating and living well is never really over. As you age, your nutritional needs and taste preferences may change. Some foods won't fit your diet plan anymore because you will make lifestyle changes, or your health will require you to incorporate different foods into your dietary regimen. Once you become more confident in the kitchen and familiar with a wider variety of foods, adjusting to your new diet will evolve naturally. Who knows where your journey will go, as you carry on the process of self-discovery and the creation of your own *recipe for a healthy life!*

INDEX

FOOTNOTES

[1] Mateljan, George. *The World's Healthiest Foods: Essential Guide for the Healthiest Way of Eating.* Seattle: GMF Publishing. 2007. P. 86.

[2] United States Department of Agriculture. "How Many Vegetables Are Needed Daily or Weekly?" <http://www. choosemyplate.gov/printpages/MyPlateFoodGroups/Vegetables/food-groups.vegetables-amount.pdf>.

[3] Perlmutter, David. *Grain Brain.* New York: Little, Brown and Company. 2013. P. 32.

[4] Ludvigsson, Jonas F., Daniel A. Leffler, Julio C. Bai, Federico Biagi, Alessio Fasano, et al. "The Oslo Definitions for Coeliac Disease and Related Terms." *Gut Online.* Feb 16, 2012. Vol. 62, no. 1, pp. 43-52. <http://gut.bmj.com/content/62/1/43. full?sid=918fd8f0-bed7-4695-a274-0b102c2ce847>.

[5] Lieberman, Shari. *The Gluten Connection: How Gluten Sensitivity May Be Sabotaging Your Health—And What You Can Do to Take Control Now.* New York: Rodale Books. 2007. P. 2.

[6] Wangen, Stephen. *Healthier Without Wheat: A New Understanding of Wheat Allergies, Celiac Disease, and Non-Celiac Gluten Intolerance.* Seattle: Innate Health Publishing. 2009. P. 37.

[7] If you would like to get tested, I recommend Entero Lab and Cyrex Labs, facilities that offer reliable state-of-the-art technology to diagnose gluten intolerance: www.enterolab.com and www.cyrexlabs. com.

[8] Natural Resources Defense Council. "Mercury Contamination in Fish: A Guide to Staying Healthy and Fighting Back." <http://www.nrdc.org/health/effects/mercury/guide.asp>.

[9] Food Marketing Institute. *The Food Keeper.* Food Marketing Institute. 2014. <www.fmi.org/food-keeper>.

[10] Stanchich, Lino. *Power Eating Program: You Are How You Eat.* Healthy Products, Inc. 1989. Pp. 47-48.

[11] Ibid. Pp. 67, 76.

[12] Porter, Jessica. *The Hip Chick's Guide to Macrobiotics: A Philosophy for Achieving a Radiant Mind and a Fabulous Body.* Avery. 2004. Pp. 82-83.

[13] United States Department of Agriculture. "Chapter 2: Profiling Food Consumption in America." *Agriculture Fact Book 2001-2002.* United States Department of Agriculture. 2003. Pp. 13-21. <http://www. usda.gov/factbook/ chapter2.pdf>.

[14] Bentley, Jeanine and Jean Buzby. "Caloric Sweeteners: Per capita availability adjusted for loss." United States Department of Agriculture, Economic Research Service. 2014.

23890035R00052

Made in the USA
San Bernardino, CA
05 September 2015